"In *Untouchable*, Brittany takes Ernest Hemingway's idea, to write hard and clear about what hurts, to the limit. In doing so, she exposes her greatest struggles as a harbinger so others can avoid the traps of ignorance and unpreparedness—and instead experience God's unflinching protection, grace and love."

Kirk Noonan, chief visioneer, Left Field Innovation Lab

"I am honored to know Brittany and to have had the privilege of being a part of this beautiful story of hope and redemption. As she opens up the secret places of her heart to touch yours, the rawness and honesty of her words will captivate your attention. The message of this book is so needed, not only for those who are experiencing the pain and consequences of sexual sin, but for those who desire to keep from experiencing that pain. I believe Brittany's story and her dynamic biblical insight offer a fresh and much-needed perspective on failure and restoration that everyone needs to hear!"

Debbie Lindell, lead pastor, James River Church;
author, *She Believes*

"I love courageous people! I (probably like most of you) am a sucker for stories of unbridled courage. As I've gotten older and have become a passionate student of human behavior, I've come to this conclusion about courage: The highest form of courage is vulnerability. *Untouchable* is a beautiful and courageous cautionary tale of how easy it is to fall, precisely when you think you are standing firm. Brittany's vulnerability about her own struggle and weakness is refreshing. It's a cup of cold water to a dry and weary soul. Read it. You won't regret it."

Chad Bruegman, directional leader and teaching pastor,
Red Rocks Church

UNTOUCHABLE

Unraveling the Myth That You're Too Faithful to Fall

BRITTANY RUST

Chosen

a division of Baker Publishing Group
Minneapolis, Minnesota

© 2018 by Brittany Rust

Published by Chosen Books
11400 Hampshire Avenue South
Bloomington, Minnesota 55438
www.chosenbooks.com

Chosen Books is a division of
Baker Publishing Group, Grand Rapids, Michigan

Printed in the United States of America

ISBN 978-0-8007-9880-2
Library of Congress Control Number: 2017963659

The story about Sgt. Timothy Gilboe in chapter 9 is taken from "Shot at Point Blank Range" by Lisa Ferdinando and used by permission of the U.S. Army News Service.

Personal stories of individuals in this book are used by permission. Identifying details of certain individuals have been changed to protect their privacy.

Cover design by Emily Weigel

Author is represented by The Steve Laube Agency.

18 19 20 21 22 23 24   7 6 5 4 3 2 1

No one has captivated my heart like You have.
No one has been as good to me as You have.
And no one has faithfully stood by my side as You have.
You *didn't* give up on me, even when I gave up on You.
You loved me even when I didn't love myself.

Your love and great sacrifice are the most beautiful gifts
I could ever receive, and I am eternally grateful.
You made redemption possible and brought me to it
entirely because You decided before time began
that You would love Your daughter
in spite of her reckless attempt to do life on her own.
Truly nobody has my heart like You do,
and this is all for You.

If any change or impact is made
in people's hearts, it is Your doing.
Thank You for allowing me to be a part of it.

Contents

Foreword

Too many Christians, especially those in ministry, believe they are untouchable—that they are too faithful to fall or too spiritual to give in to temptation. They deny any sort of weakness, fail to draw proper boundaries and end up doing the very things they swore they would never do.

Pastor and author Brittany Rust was one such person—until she found herself in the middle of a moral failure and a church-wide scandal. Bewildered, humiliated and ashamed, she thought she was beyond redemption. But God's grace met her on the ground, and here she shares what she has learned through her painful journey. She unravels the myth of being untouchable, showing how we start to believe the lie, and how we can protect ourselves from temptation. Ultimately she shows that to truly flourish in life, you must be willing to admit weakness—and that no one is beyond God's redeeming love.

Bianca Juarez Olthoff, founder, In the Name of Love Ministries

Acknowledgments

To my handsome husband, Ryan, this story is not my own. It is yours as well, and you have always given me permission and grace to share it. Thank you for being my biggest cheerleader and loving me through it all. Not only have you given me space to share and dream, but you have also provided the encouragement to be the best version of myself. I truly couldn't have done this without you.

To my dear son, Roman, this book was birthed as you were, too. You softened my heart when you made me your mama and allowed me to be more vulnerable in sharing parts of my story I previously held in secrecy. You gave me the courage to let my walls down so that others might, too. I pray you will always know that regardless of the mistakes you might make, His grace is sufficient and redemption is possible.

To my family and friends who walked the journey of redemption with me, thank you for your unwavering support in the valley. People like you don't come around very often, and I am where I am today because of your love.

To you, the reader, I say this: Dare to be vulnerable. Have the courage to live in weakness. And never doubt the immense love and grace you have access to through Christ Jesus. This labor of love is for you.

Introduction

I had never been so anxious or nervous in my whole life. I sat at a large conference table at the church where I worked, with ladies I had worked with for many years, tears streaming down my face. My heart beat so fast and so hard it felt as if it could burst out of my chest at any moment. I was terrified of the turn my life was about to take.

These were godly women I admired deeply, and I knew I was about to disappoint them with my shocking news. I had fallen—fallen further than I ever imagined, and all because of a moment of weakness. I had done something I never thought I would do. But I will share more about that a bit later.

Flashback to my early twenties and the eager Christian girl I was. Eager to be uncompromisable, undaunted but, more than anything, untouchable. I set out to serve the Kingdom of God wholeheartedly and to help build our local church with purity and passion. I sought wise mentors, was at my church every moment the doors were open and read as many nonfiction Christian books as I could get my hands on. It was exactly what I needed after years of living separated from God, depressed and in bondage to more than one stronghold. In that incubator I learned a lot, for which I am grateful. There was something missing, though, that only postfailure could I put my finger on. I now call it "the untouchable myth."

I had a list of things I would never do, a list I adopted from mentors, friends, teachers and the Word of God. *I would never get drunk. I would never cheat or steal. I would never purposely hurt someone. I would never have sex outside of marriage.* The list went on. I put the possibility of ever compromising or giving in to these temptations completely out of my mind. *I would never,* so I rarely thought about my list. Why do anything to guard against sin I would obviously (in my mind) never commit? This was my biggest mistake.

Because I never accepted the possibility of compromise, I never properly guarded myself and established the boundaries I needed to avoid the very things I said I would never do. As a result, at the age of 25 I committed a sin that cost me everything. The most obvious cost—a certain purity and hoped-for abstinence. On the heels of that were shame, guilt and a sense of diminished intimacy with God. It cost me years of ministry sowed and a dream job. It also cost me credibility, my boyfriend, relationships and trust. I had never lost so much, and the cost had never been so high—to this day that still stands true.

What is this idea I call "the untouchable myth," and why should you guard against it?

It is a mentality, an idea, a façade. This myth is the belief that nothing can touch you. Or at least that certain sins or acts can never touch you. It is a lie that pulls you in and holds you in invisible bondage. It tells you not to worry about guarding yourself because "of course" you would never do that thing or commit that sin. So because you buy into this lie, you think you live in freedom. Freedom from what you have determined you will never do. Freedom to live out of your own strength. But it is a mirage in the desert of bondage.

The truth is, ignoring something does not give you more freedom; in fact, it keeps you in bondage. Bondage to false hope and self-reliance. Bondage that keeps you hidden in the shadows instead of basking in the light. This is not the way you want to live, and you do not have to.

Are there sins you believe adamantly you will never commit? Things you are sure you can stand firmly against? Most likely, yes. It is natural to assume you would not do something that in your mind seems wrong. *Sexual immorality. Addiction. Rage. Theft.* The list goes on.

Odds are pretty good that you have a list of untouchables; many people do. But your defense stops at the list. No further action is taken, and the myth creates a foothold for sin. How do you conquer an untouchable mindset and shatter the myth? You have to accept one thing: weakness.

By not admitting weakness, you leave room for it; by believing you are untouchable, you become vulnerable to failure. Truth is, we are all more impressionable than we would like to admit. It takes only a certain amount of pressure under the right circumstances to do what you never thought possible. This is weakness that is often difficult to accept, a hard pill to swallow for the devoted Christian.

Not only because you are a believer, but more so because God has placed a unique calling on your life, the enemy has placed a target on you. You can block the possibility of moral failure from your mind and remain vulnerable to his attacks, or you can accept that you are not untouchable and take an active part in preparing yourself against temptation.

In the first two chapters, I will share my own story of having an untouchable mentality, yet finding myself exactly where I thought I would never be—on the other end of moral failure. It is a cautionary tale of epic proportions; you won't want to miss it! I will also explore the origins of the myth for me and how it can arise in your own life. Then, throughout the book, we will dive into what I have learned about the myth.

As we explore the truth about the myth, you can read about how this mentality can actually hurt you, and how living with a mindset of admitting weakness is really one of the best things you can do for yourself. We will continue the journey through the death of the myth, where you will find practical tools for overcoming such a mindset. And if you have suffered an "epic fail," as I did, we will continue with recovery so that you can find your way to redemption. Finally, we will wrap it up by looking at church discipline and ways you can help someone else who has made a bit of a mess of his or her life.

At the end of each chapter you will find a few questions to help you explore more deeply the ways the content might apply to you and draw out what God might be communicating to your heart. I will also include a short closing prayer to help guide your prayers in relation to the content we are diving into. I pray you will take these questions and closing prayers into a few moments of quiet time and go on a heart search. Create the space for God to speak tenderly to you and help you work through your own potential untouchable mindset. This book will only be helpful if you give yourself time and margin to process what God is wanting to do in your life.

Oh, and then my handsome husband, Ryan, will share his perspective of the story and what he learned, so stick around to the end!

So, why should you care to keep reading? To hear a story of how bright-eyed hope can lead to rock-bottom ache. To find out how the untouchable myth might be playing a role in your life without your even knowing it. And to get the tools you need to overcome the myth so that you can flourish in the calling placed on your life.

Are you willing to take this journey so that you can come out of it more resilient? Then head to the next page!

Part 1

THE ORIGIN
OF THE MYTH

1

Bright-Eyed and Untouchable

Therefore, if anyone is in Christ, the new creation has come: The old has gone, the new is here!

2 Corinthians 5:17 NIV

One of my earliest memories in life is sexual. I was four or five years old and remember very little about what happened—other than it took place in a dark room. Rather, it was the aftermath of how I dealt with the experience that I remember most. That experience was the root for the thing I struggled with most in life—a bondage that had me in its firm grip for as long as I could remember. And even as I write this, having been set free for many years now, I wonder if I am truly free from its hold on my life. I say that because God is prompting me to share something with you I have never shared with anyone but my husband. And while I sense God's prompting to be vulnerable with you, I am scared. In fact, I am terrified of what you and others might think of me. And that fear of shame begs me to ask myself: Am I truly free from the bondage if I cannot live in the freedom to share it?

So right now, with you as a witness to this very personal moment for me, I am asking God to break that last chain of bondage as I share my story. All of it—every dark and messy part—so that God can use it to help others who might be in a similar place. I no longer want to be afraid or ashamed of the past; I want God to be magnified in the transformation that has taken place in my life and for others, perhaps you, to feel the same freedom to shake off the chains entangling you. So, here I go.

I was sexually abused as a child by someone outside of my immediate family. While that prompts in many a fear of anything sexual, it had the opposite effect on me. Instead of fearing men or wanting to avoid sexual activity, I grew up with an addiction to masturbation and pornography. (Even typing this now sends shivers of fear down my spine for sharing this openly!) For years I struggled with something that always left me feeling empty and ashamed. For years I tried to stop an addiction I could not shake, feeling guilty and resolving never to do something so perverted again. For years I lived in sexual bondage, without any hope of freedom in sight. I was a slave to sin.

It was this struggle that became my greatest vulnerability. It was the ball and chain holding me back, keeping me anchored in the shadows of guilt. And it did, in fact, cause my greatest downfall. But we will get to that later on.

I grew up in a large middle-class family—the only girl and the oldest of four—in the Midwest. I had a relatively average American upbringing of playing outside with the neighborhood kids in the evening, eating spaghetti and tacos for dinner and spending hours on the family Super Nintendo system. What I did not have, however, was any understanding of God. I had no idea there was this beautiful Creator out there longing to capture my heart and set me free. Our family did not go to church, and I have no recollection of conversations about God or faith. I was told that if you are a good person you will go to heaven; that was all I knew, and I had no reason to believe otherwise. Yet even then I knew that masturbation and pornography were wrong, that they were not honorable. Even with the unbiblical mindset I had as someone who did not know Christ and who believed I just had to be a good person, those acts still rang of perversion. Nothing seemed right about what I was doing.

I love my parents and have incredible respect for them, but childhood was not always easy for me or my oldest brother. My parents both have tragic stories they have had to deal with; I cannot begin to imagine how hard their own childhoods were. Unfortunately, though, what they struggled with inwardly got expressed outwardly in our home—mostly as anger, anger that was seen in furious action and felt in subtle tension. It was such a huge part of my environment that I came to embrace it as my own. For years I would easily lose my temper, fly off the handle, be short with people and get into some intense physical matches with my brothers that included breaking down doors. It was not pretty.

Because of the sexual bondage and anger issues, I lived in a very dark world. I felt alone and lost for many years. I never knew life could be better, but some deep part of me hoped for the possibility. To explain the heaviness I carried with me is a challenge, but I always felt as though some dark weight was upon me—an oppression of sorts. It felt like a massive, invisible chain locked around me and weighing me down. No matter how hard I tried, I could not break free from its grasp.

I would fail in my resolve to stop doing those shameful acts and hate myself. I would get into yet another heated discussion with my dad and end up feeling that I was never good enough. I would hit my younger brother when tensions were high and experience quiet guilt. I was a failure; that was my belief about myself. I could not and probably would not ever measure up in life.

In high school I began struggling with depression, and in those dark moments my thoughts turned to suicide. I never took action, but I sometimes thought it would all be easier if I were not alive. If I were gone, there would be nothing, no pain, no burden to carry alone any longer.

Sadly, I think that is an easy place for many people to go to when life is hard. Oftentimes people who are in pain and without hope either go numb through self-medication with drugs, drinking and sex, or they cope through cutting (self-mutilation), both of which provide a false sense of temporary relief. Ultimately, people in pain want to escape to a place where the pain is gone, or at least secondary. They lack hope, and without hope life seems too heavy a burden to carry. I get that, and if that is you now, you are not alone in how you feel.

In spite of all that was going on, I wanted to believe there was more. When I went to those dark corners in my mind, I somehow would begin to hope for something better. For a long time, hope in a better life was the only thing that got me through the hard times. I think this is where my optimism was birthed—the part of me that fueled a strong drive to move forward in spite of the unlovely circumstances. Perhaps I leaned too much on that optimism. It played into my untouchable mentality, but we will get to that a bit later.

My depression and emotional heaviness came to a head one night when I woke up in agony. I crawled to my parents' room with the worst pain I had known up till that point. They took me to the doctor, and I was told I was on the verge of an ulcer. At the age of sixteen, I was put on various medications, including one for depression. So not only was I struggling with sexual bondage, anger and depression, but now I was medicating. My life had never been so empty and without purpose.

I knew I was lost.

A New Season

Not long after the ulcer incident, a friend invited me to a youth service at a nearby church. I went, mostly to get out of the house and to be with kids my own age, but I found that night the very thing I had been looking for all my life: real, tangible hope. Not the false hope I had conjured up in my hardship, but real hope that could shine a spotlight on my emptiness and illuminate the darkness.

I remember exactly where I was sitting when God called my name that Wednesday night: on the aisle, in the middle, toward the back. The house lights were low while the stage lights pierced through the room with rays of optimism in the darkness. Heads were bowed as the worship team played softly behind the youth pastor's powerful call to the altar.

I will be honest; although I knew that hope was possible, I was nervous to take that step out of my seat—out of the hiddenness I lived in—and walk down to the altar. I was surrounded by many of my high school peers and I was afraid of what they would think. Would they laugh at my vulnerability the next day? But the call of the Father, the sacrifice of Jesus and the message of the Gospel compelled me out of my fear and obscurity, and into a new relationship with God. My fears and nerves were no match for the excitement in my heart to start anew!

I began a conversation with God in that hidden moment, with eyes closed, and continued it down the aisle and to the altar that night. I unloaded all my shame, fears and doubts at the foot of the cross and made a commitment that I would follow Him all the days of my life. I told Him I loved Him and that He had all of me.

As I laid it all out before Him and made Jesus Christ my Savior, despair and hopelessness began to evaporate into nothing. My hope in Him and eternity took root. I believed God had the power to transform my heart, soul and mind in truly powerful ways.

Amazingly, God saw a wreck of a sixteen-year-old girl struggling with some very dark matters who would go on to make great mistakes. He did not look past me; He saw me. Saw every part of me and still wanted me for His own.

When I heard the Gospel that night, I knew I was hearing truth—something real and transformative—and I wanted it. I wanted Him. And so that night I gave my life over to the One who loved me more than anyone else could. I traded in my ashes for beauty, my sin for redemption. I found eternal hope in the love of the Father.

My life took a turn that day; I began to change for the better. I was delivered instantly from depression and experienced the power God has to transform someone's life. With this change I also no longer needed the medications I had been using to keep my sadness and stress at bay. Now, granted, I was not magically set free from hardship—I still had strongholds, and I still faced dark times. But God began to shatter my current beliefs about myself and my life, transforming me to be more like Him.

After that night I spent as much time at my church as I could. My two best friends both committed their lives to Christ not long after, which helped us all be more accountable. I also began to make other godly friends and experience an environment that was not dark and angry. My life began to look a bit brighter.

After I finished high school I became a youth leader at church. That first year I watched God begin to work out the strongholds of sex and anger I carried. I struggled with both after salvation, but then at separate times God radically moved in both areas as I pursued Him with all my heart. The shackles began to break, and freedom became tangible. Less guilt and more room to breathe; more room to grow and flourish.

It goes to show that God can deliver us from any addiction, stronghold or burden. I was becoming a living testimony of that! I knew it was the power of God alone that was setting me free. I tried to keep my heart focused on walking in the light and radically pursuing His love.

And I did this with incredible vigor and excitement. I enrolled in the church's nine-month discipleship program where, along with other young Millennials like myself, I served at the church in full-time volunteer ministry, put in hours of prayer and Bible study and drew as close to God as I could get.

That season in my life led to a real growth spurt. I began to mature quickly in that incubator of hope, accountability and modeled leadership. I learned how to study the Bible, pray and serve. It was at this time I preached a sermon for a class assignment and discovered that I have passion for studying and communicating the Word of God. It set me on a trajectory I have kept since. Slowly my unhealthy mindset began to change. I was building a foundation for a thriving future both as a believer and as someone pursuing vocational ministry—meaning working for a Christian organization in ways that best used the gifts God had placed in my life. It was one of the most transformational seasons I have ever experienced.

It was also the season when the untouchable myth started to take shape for me. It was not a conscious decision, just a gradual sense that I was too faithful ever to fall.

The Birth of the Untouchable

When I was twenty years old and offered a job at my church after the completion of the discipleship program, I was unaware of the challenges—not only of entering vocational ministry but also of navigating life as a young believer. I had some struggles, particularly while still living in a home that did not share my beliefs, but I thought that once I got out on my own, life would be a breeze. In fact, it was for a bit. With that and how much I was growing at the church, I believed life would only get easier. The life of a believer is supposed to be easy, right?

I know I am not the only one who has believed this. Many people—perhaps even you—enter a relationship with God and imagine that life will now have less hardship. But if you have not already figured this out, the Christian walk is not like that. The enemy sees someone he wants back under his reign and, with this target on your back, he will pursue your soul to an even greater degree. But I did not understand this quite yet. I went into Christianity bright-eyed and feeling untouchable. I believed that because I was a believer called to vocational ministry, I was on an easy path. Furthermore, I began to believe that nothing could get me down. I had been to a very low place in life and had no intention of ever returning. I could only go up from there, right?

Pair this false outlook on life with intense optimism and you get me in my early twenties. As I began to grow spiritually and spend more time in a Christian environment, I began to adopt a list of things I should and should not do. I should pray, read my Bible, go to church, serve others, etc. In contrast, I should not do drugs, lie, steal, have sex outside of marriage, etc. Any of this sound familiar? It was my list of what I call "untouchables," and because by my very nature I lean toward a black-and-white perspective, I left no room for compromise. This was how I saw it, how it was and how it would be.

Here is what happened to me in my experience of compiling a list of untouchables and what I believe many Christians are struggling with. I had my list of things I would never do because I knew they were wrong; the Bible made this clear. What I did, though, was take those actions, set them up on a shelf, shut the cupboard door and never think about them again. In my mind the untouchables were clearly wrong, so I assumed I would never do them, which is why I tucked them far away. But because I never thought about them, I fell into the untouchable myth trap: I failed to guard myself against these very things.

Why guard myself against something I would "never do"?

Much like Peter in his story of denying Jesus before the crucifixion (which we will learn more about in chapter 4), we convince ourselves that we will never do certain things, those acts so beneath or unlike us that we completely put them out of mind. *It is because we avoid accepting the fact that they are even a possibility that we become vulnerable to the very things we said we would never do.*

Why is it we hear so many stories of pastors falling into moral failure or people we look up to as mighty men and women of

29

God getting caught up in sin we could never imagine they would commit? We are shocked at such stories. Honestly, no reputable pastors go into ministry believing they will steal from their congregations or fall into affairs. No strong believers imagine that after years of faithful servanthood they will get caught up in an addiction. Because they fail to accept sin as a possibility and fail to put the proper guardrails in place, they become vulnerable to the temptation.

You, I am sure, have no intention of going down a dark path of sin and failure, but that does not mean you won't.

Happy and Content

That is where I was in my twenties. I was pursuing the calling of God on my life with optimism and fearlessness. I found incredible purpose and passion in what I was doing, loving every aspect. It was a life I could not have conceived of in my depression before I became a Christian. I was being blessed to serve with a team of women who were growing one of the largest women's ministries in the country. God was starting to use my passion for His Word through writing and opportunities to speak around the Midwest. Furthermore, I was trusted by my church family, one of the greatest gifts in the world.

God was using me in ways I had never dreamed possible, and with my list of untouchables safely out of sight, I felt confident that I would never stumble or falter in my path. My mindset was firm.

I was that twenty-something professional with lots of wonderful friends, a vibrant social life and a fantastic job. I was happy and content. But one thing was missing, that one thing most people are looking for: companionship.

Before the age of 25, I had never been in a relationship. I had dated some guys but never really had a boyfriend. I will share with you what came next in chapter 2, where it all changed for me, and you will get a glimpse into my epic fail. In addition, over the next two chapters we will dive deeper into the untouchable myth so that you can get a better idea of how it could play out in your life. Once I have shared my story and broken down the myth, we are going to start building a stronger foundation as we explore how the myth can be a hindrance to your own walk with God. If you and I truly want to flourish in life, we must be willing to admit weakness. Once we have set that foundation, I have practical tools to help you guard against this untouchable mentality.

So, what does someone with an untouchable mindset look and sound like? Truth is, we come in many shapes, sizes and colors. Our untouchables are unique to us, and we tuck them away in different places. In general, though, this person is someone who does not accept the thought that certain sins are possible to commit—even those she might label as the worst of sins. It is the person who says "I'll never" do that. It is the believer who assumes he is above falling into the untouchables.

I believe the majority of believers has an untouchable mentality. Some will barely escape falling, but, reality is, most will fall. Most will end up doing something they say they would never do. This is not for lack of wanting to refrain from sin but rather a result of not being prepared to stand firm against it. So to you, the reader, I say this: You are not untouchable. You are not exempt from stumbling down an unexpected path and into an untouchable sin just because you believe it could never happen. You may very well be headed for failure you could never imagine.

The good news is, you do not have to go there. I want to walk through this journey with you so that you do not have to go through what I went through. I am praying you reach the end of this book with the tools and mindset necessary to be victorious over temptation.

Perhaps you are reading this as one who has already stumbled into the arena of sin and who is now looking for healing on the other side. Maybe you are in a place where you feel unredeemable; you believe you have made too much of a mess with your life. I want to help you walk through that journey as well—the journey to redemption. There are practical tools and tips in this book that will help you navigate away from the untouchable myth and into a healthy, vibrant life!

─────────────| GOING DEEPER |─────────────

1. Are there strongholds from your past that you have had victory over, much as I did? What are those past struggles, and possibly even current struggles, that you know you must guard against? List them for awareness and resolve today never to stop being diligent in creating space between them and you.

2. Do you have your own list of untouchables you have tucked away out of sight? Now make a list of those sins. Are you willing to be honest with yourself that you are not untouchable in these areas? Willing to expose weakness so that you might flourish?

⊣ CLOSING PRAYER ⊢

Father, I thank You that You see my past, present and future and still call me Your own. That You desire intimacy with me more than anything. I resolve to offer all I am to You. Please help me to walk this journey before me with integrity and devotion. I realize I cannot do it on my own and humbly ask that You would strengthen me by Your mighty power to be above reproach. Give me the courage to be honest about my struggles and temptations so that I don't tuck them away. I want to be open to Your working in my life today and every day after. If You have anything for me to gather from this book, I ask You to give me eyes to see what that is. Please help me to combat the untouchable myth and overcome sin by the victory Christ already obtained on the cross. Amen.

2

Then Comes the Fall

"Watch and pray that you may not enter into temptation.
The spirit indeed is willing, but the flesh is weak."

Matthew 26:41

It was Easter Sunday 2010 and an absolutely perfect spring day. I was working busily all morning at church and had been invited to an Easter luncheon of mostly singles in our twenties and thirties at a friend's house that afternoon. I was not expecting anything out of the ordinary; I figured I would know most of the people there and have a great time in easy conversation with people I had talked to a dozen times before. I was not expecting my life to change forever.

When I arrived at lunch fashionably late, I did, in fact, recognize most of the faces. As I scanned the room, however, I noticed a new face in the back, by the kitchen. I watched him for a few moments and saw that the people surrounding him seemed to be captivated by what he was saying. For this introvert it was very attractive how he lit up the room. He was tall, handsome and apparently very interesting. I took notice.

This guy and I wound up sitting next to each other, and a conversation over our shared interest in a particular theologian was sparked. I learned his name was Ryan, and I was intrigued. In fact, I remember leaving the house intrigued in a way I had never been before. The next day he sent me a Facebook friend request and our story began!

We shared the same circle of friends, and over the next few months we began to get to know each other better on those humid Missouri evenings. We had great conversations over sushi on Wednesday nights with our friends after church, sat next to each other at the movies and lingered behind the group playing putt-putt so we could have time to ourselves. Our attraction to each other seemed evident. I felt it the moment he turned around and fought a massive exiting crowd at a Fourth of July event to come and say good-bye to me. Something was brewing!

Four months after we met, Ryan said he wanted to share some personal things with me. I was extremely nervous; what was he going to say? Was it good or bad? A thousand thoughts ran through my mind. But I never expected to hear what I heard next.

Ryan told me that he had strong feelings for me (whew!), and that he needed to tell me something important about his past. He then told me that he had been married before—not once, but twice. By the age of 27, Ryan had been divorced twice.

Certainly not what I was expecting to hear! And certainly not the fairy tale every girl dreams of. I mean, I was thrilled to hear those words that told of his feelings for me, but I was completely blown away by his confession of divorce. And to be honest, up till that point my black-and-white nature would have compelled me to walk away. That is the advice I would have given any girlfriend of mine. It was a messy story, and for a conservative Christian girl in ministry, messy is not desirable. But there was something different about him. I felt conflicted—less black and white.

Still, some would call me crazy or blinded and urge me to flee from the complicated situation I was facing. And until that day I would have agreed with them. In my relationships with other men I had always come up to a red light at some point, stopping me from exploring anything further. Men with less complicated pasts, should we say. And now here was this guy with the most complicated past I had ever run across, and the red light was nowhere in sight. In my head this made no sense, but in my heart I felt peace.

After sharing my own feelings for him, I ended that conversation by expressing my appreciation for his honesty. We agreed to spend the next two weeks fasting and praying, and then we joined up at a quaint coffee shop in Springfield to talk about where we were. For my part I told him that I had a green light for the first time in my life. Which is why when he asked me out, I said yes!

The next few months were some of the most fun I had ever had. We sat under the stars for hours, talking about everything that came to mind. We went to concerts and baseball games and took day trips to Kansas City. Ryan and I got along well. I could talk to him in a way I never could talk with anyone before. It seemed right, and I felt safe with him. I was sure this guy was the guy I would marry.

Doing the Unimaginable

Then our relationship took a turn. Remember how I told you in the last chapter I thought I had been delivered from a sexual stronghold? Well, that was mostly the case. Parts of that stronghold, like the masturbation and pornography, had disappeared, but deep down inside I still carried vulnerability to anything sexual. Little did I know that the sexual temptation one experiences in a relationship was such an easy trap for me to fall into.

One night what started out as a kiss slid into more. I ended up doing something I never thought I would do: have sex outside of marriage. And just like that, an untouchable had been committed. I had gone where I never thought possible.

At first my mind went blank out of pure shock. I lay there in disbelief of what had just happened; I was not quite sure it was even real. The moment seemed to freeze; time stood still in the aftermath of my sin. But then, as if a dam let loose, thoughts began to flood my mind.

How did this happen; how did I end up here?
What will happen next?
What will this mean for our relationship?
Will God forgive me?

I cared deeply for Ryan, but this was not what I wanted for us. I wanted a pure relationship. Then the shame set in. A dark and heavy shame like nothing I had experienced before, even in all my failures before salvation. Instantly I felt far from God, as if my sin had placed a gap between us. That night I went home feeling lost and unsure for the first time in a long time.

The next day I shared what had happened with one of my close friends. Talking with someone who both cared for me and had a strong foundation in God helped me process what had happened and what I needed to do next.

My friend responded lovingly and boldly. She helped me find the courage to step forward and confess to my pastors. I was ready to go into work the next day and bring my sin into the light.

That is not how it went, though. As much as I would have liked to have stepped forward first, my friend grew nervous over the news and, before I arrived, told my pastor's wife, who was also my boss and mentor. So before I had the opportunity to confess, my pastors knew what had happened.

I stepped into the office that day and was asked point-blank if Ryan and I had had sex. In that moment I was shattered emotionally and spiritually into a million pieces. The weight of what I had done seemed to take on more heaviness as I shared with my pastor's wife what had happened. Not only was I ashamed of myself and feeling far from God, but now I was disappointing people who had poured so much into me over the years. I could see the disappointment on her face. Yet I could blame no one but myself; I was the one who had fallen.

My pastor's wife, once I had shared it all with her, proceeded to tell me I could no longer serve on the women's ministry team, in leadership or anywhere else within the church. I was stripped of my ministry responsibilities and my job—work I had poured my heart into for the past seven years. I was then brought into two separate meetings that morning to confess what I had done to groups of people I worked with. I sat there with tears streaming down my face as I told the women's ministry team what had happened. Some of these women were my closest friends as well, so although it was a safe place, again, I was deeply ashamed.

That day I did a lot of confessing. That day I also lost the opportunity for any church ministry, at least for a while. The speaking engagements went away. I stopped writing for a season. I was stripped of all the things that I was passionate about—that made me feel alive.

Fortunately I had loving pastors and friends to walk me through the journey. Although I could no longer serve as part of the women's ministry, I was encouraged to continue attending the church, which I did. I found incredible grace and support there; I experienced healing in the presence of God and restoration through their godly support.

In addition, God was there to carry me through the aftermath season and provide for all my needs. I was able to nanny for a wonderful godly family; kids I adore to this day! I also worked part-time as a receptionist with a nonprofit organization that turned into a wonderful full-time job for many years. I might have made a huge mistake that cost me so much professionally, but God began an immediate work of taking care of me and starting my journey over again.

That day of confession also became a turning point in my relationship with Ryan. At the end of that day, I was completely drained; I had never cried so much before. I called Ryan and could hear the care and concern in his voice. Honestly, at that point I thought he was the only one I could turn to. He came and picked me up, and we talked a lot that night. It was there, in seeing his care and his heart for me, that I knew I loved this man.

Still, as close as we felt in that moment, it did not make what had happened easier. You see, there is a reason sex is meant to be saved for marriage. Sexual intimacy takes a piece of you and your heart away. It is given to someone else, whether you want it to be or not. A piece you can never get back. Dating couples who have sex often find that it adds pressure they are not ready for.

Our relationship became too serious to be comfortable after that. Having lost so much, I turned to Ryan to fill what was gone. And because we had been together intimately and I loved him, I thought that meant we *needed* to get more serious. I had just given him a piece of me I only ever wanted to give my husband. The relationship was propelled forward before either of us was ready.

The pressure was a lot to handle. And the sexual desires did not go away. After trying incredibly hard not to give in to temptation again, we did. Although I had felt the weight of my sin in every way possible and had tried not to fall again, my efforts could not transform me into a person of moral victory. So after a few months of trying to navigate the aftermath of our sin, feeling the heaviness between us and failing again, Ryan and I broke up. We were not in a healthy place and could no longer maintain the relationship.

Now, not only had I lost the ministry opportunity I was privileged to be part of, but I had lost the man I loved. No longer did I have Ryan to find refuge in, to serve as a bandage over my emotional wounds. Which left me keenly aware of what I had lost most: my intimacy with God. I was alone and feeling further away from God than ever before. In this dark place I began doing the only thing I knew to do: draw close to God and begin the rebuilding process; start walking through healing and restoration; try to put the pieces of my life back together. Most importantly, get my priorities back in check with God at the center.

I got sidetracked quickly, though. Two months later Ryan and I started dating again, thinking we had had our break and could now move forward. But it was too soon. We dated for a while and then called it quits again—but this time, for good. Marriage did not seem the best choice for two people struggling to find a healthy path to a future free from sin and shame. Marriage was not the answer to our problems; it would have made them worse. Breaking up to be better Christ-followers and versions of ourselves was the only answer. The first breakup had been hard, but I always had the idea we would get back together. To end it this time, cutting all ties, was a stake through the heart.

Heading into Darkness

In this dark season of my life, I went to new lows and found myself farther away from God than I had been since I knew Him. Those days were brutal as I weathered incredible ups and downs. I am not proud of all the ways I handled it, but my prayer is that my story will help you if you find yourself in your own stormy season.

For a while after the breakup, I tried hard to put all of my focus on God. I threw myself into following Him to get through the long days and nights. I surrounded myself with godly people and spent most of my free time (which I had a lot of) in prayer and worship. Time in His presence was about the only place I found refuge from the pain and sorrow.

But this did not stop the daily breakdowns of crying in an empty office at work or my quiet apartment. The nights were always the hardest: lying there in the dark with my thoughts racing, leading to emotional tugs at my heart. Eventually I got tired of all the crying and the little relief I felt in return. After a few months of this I became frustrated with God. Why was I not getting past this? Why was it not getting any easier? I could not understand why I was throwing myself at His feet and feeling no better than the day Ryan and I split up.

The breaking point for me came one humid night while I was out on my nightly run through downtown. I was running down the street and ran right into Ryan. I was beyond excited, and we started to chat. Being the emotional wreck that I was, I told him I missed him. Big mistake for my heart. Ryan said he was seeing someone else and that there was no way he and I would be getting back together.

I was crushed—in fact, devastated. Up until that point, I had held on to some small belief we would find our way back to each other, eventually. But that hope was finally smothered. He had a new life apart from me.

That is when I hit my rock bottom, the darkest season of my entire life. I made a decision that night that I am not proud of. I decided to give my pain and healing over to the world. I was not walking away from God; I still loved Him. But I had been trying His way and going nowhere, so I figured I would try getting past Ryan the same way many people do.

The world tells the broken and hurting that healing comes from a Band-Aid of relationships, alcohol and escape by any means possible. Listening to this lie, I would go on a date or two with multiple guys, Christian or not, to mask my loneliness. One Friday night I felt so alone and sad that I drank a whole bottle of wine in my apartment and texted Ryan something I feel sure was entirely sappy and embarrassing. I even contemplated suicide one night to escape the pain.

My life was a hot mess. In that isolating darkness and unfulfilled healing, I broke once more. But I broke the right way—in a good way this time. I had known the world's way would never work even before I tried it, but sometimes we are not quite smart enough to go with what we know. After trying the wrong way of getting through a breakup, I recommitted myself to the healing process God's way. And healing truly did begin to take place.

Turning Page

Looking back, I can see now that when I initially sought healing after breaking up with Ryan I went about it all wrong. My prayers sounded something like this: *God, make the pain go away* or *God, please speed up the process.* The intention behind my prayers was not true healing and restoration but a quick fix. I wanted to get around the pain or rush through it. Yet true healing of the heart comes through time and patience. I was never going to get the healing I was hoping and praying for by rushing through the season.

I want to pause for a moment and speak to you because perhaps you have tried to rush through your own healing. Maybe even now. But let me assure you: Proper healing will never come if you try to rush through or get around the pain. You must face it head on.

Did you know that buffalo run right into a storm? Unlike cattle, and most living things for that matter, that run away from an approaching storm, buffalo make a charge toward it. By running away, cattle spend more time in the storm because they cannot outrun it. But buffalo run right for it, and by facing it and going through it, they actually spend less time in discomfort.

What I was trying to do, and what many people do, was outrun the storm. When I decided to turn and face it head on, God began to bring me through it. I finally started seeing restoration take place.

As I began healing, I let go of Ryan. I let go of a dream of what our lives could be like together. I began to find restoration and healing from the sin I had engaged in and the subsequent shame. Most importantly, I started finding intimacy with God again. It was hard, yes, but it was worth it to experience proper healing through the power of grace and redemption in Christ Jesus.

Those next few months were difficult, but they were sweet. I stopped dating and pursuing any idea of what the world labels as healing, put God first and, most importantly, sought proper restoration. I sought a healing that did not come from bypassing the pain but from facing it head on. God was mending my heart and bringing restoration to my brokenness—redeeming that season of my life. I had truly let go of Ryan in pursuit of healing and felt soothing calmness come over me.

Then God did the unexpected. When I was truly able to lay down the thing I held most dear and finally look to Him alone for restoration, He gave back to me what I loved.

Seven months after Ryan and I broke up, we reconnected when a mutual friend told him that someone had tried to break into my apartment. My dad gave me a gun after the incident, and Ryan called one day and offered to take me to a shooting range to teach me how to use it.

That started a new chapter for us, as we had lengthy (and hard) conversations about our past and present over long dinners. Within a month we decided to begin dating again with the intention of doing everything we could to keep our focus on God and His will for us.

After another two years of dating, Ryan proposed to me on top of a mountain in Colorado on one of the best days of my life. As the sun set over Denver, he bent down on one knee and asked me to be his wife. Three months later we got married

45

on another mountain in Colorado—near our new home in Colorado Springs—with our families and closest friends surrounding us. Some of those friends are the very girls who sat in that conference room when I confessed years before. The pastor who performed the ceremony was my counselor through that dark season. It was the full-circle moment of God's redemptive power in our lives.

God has been so good to us—restoring our relationship, allowing us both to be in ministry again and restoring our dreams. God is using me and us in ways I never imagined. I am living proof that God can take the shattered and tattered messes of our lives and piece them back together for use beyond our wildest dreams! Even better than seeing my own dreams come to fruition is watching God use our story to encourage others in their own journeys.

It took me years to tell our story, but once I knew God had redeemed it, I could not help but share it with others as a testimony to His goodness—and as a cautionary word: You are not untouchable, but you are redeemable. If you have fallen into things you consider untouchable—if you have made an epic fail—I will help you with your journey later in this book. But for now know that there can be a turning page in your story if you offer your story to God. Your epic fail is a scene in your story, but not the end of it.

GOING DEEPER

1. Are you currently trying an unhealthy method to mask pain or loneliness? With some honest reflection, if this

is true, what are those actions that you should step away from? What do you need to let go of in order to experience proper healing?

2. Do you believe that God is good and will take care of you in every season? How is He caring for you now?

O God, how great and thorough is Your care for me. You are my provider, and every good gift comes from You. I am both humbled by and grateful for Your generosity and never-ending love for me. I know I have failed You and will likely fail again, but may I never be closed off to Your loving-kindness. Please, examine my heart and show me where I'm hiding from You. Show me if there is pain I'm masking or running from. If I lack true healing anywhere, reveal it to me. I pray You would give me strength to face the pain and experience proper healing by You. Make me whole, Lord. Make me like You. Amen.

3

The Untouchable Connection

The prudent sees danger and hides himself, but the simple go on and suffer for it.

Proverbs 22:3

Jason spent his formative years as a pastor's kid. At the young age of nine, he had his first experience with pornography. In high school he began to dabble in it periodically, and it was then his dad discovered Jason's use of it. The hidden sin was never dealt with, however, which perpetuated secrecy about the struggle that would plague Jason for many years to come.

After graduating from high school, Jason embarked on a new journey by enrolling in an intern program at a church. It was a time of extraordinary growth for a young man out on his own for the first time. For the most part, Jason was able to subdue his porn addiction and keep it at bay, although one moment of weakness drove him to seek counseling. This helped for a bit, but not forever. He thought he was dealing with his secret sin, but really he was only covering it up. In his untouchable mentality, Jason tried in his own strength to put the sin behind him and walk forward in the hope he would never compromise again.

Jason was invited to stay at the church to develop his leadership capabilities, which he did. The next year he was invited to join the church leadership staff, but he turned down the position to move to another state with his new wife and serve as the youth pastor for his dad's church.

That is where Jason's hidden addiction to porn began to consume him. As he dove into full-time ministry, the youth pastor began to experience an overwhelming desire to feed the sin. Admittedly, he knew he was weak but was ashamed to share his struggle with anyone else. Besides, Jason was a pastor—a leader—so whom could he talk to about his hidden shame? He was supposed to be strong, a role model; admitting the sin did not seem like a viable option.

Seven months after taking the youth pastor position, the church where he had previously been at again asked him to come on staff as a pastor, and this time Jason accepted. Opportunities for more leadership and teaching began to open for him. It was an exciting time professionally but a terrifying time personally. Jason knew he should have dealt with his sin and wanted to be rid of the shame and guilt. The stakes were higher now, however, and the perceived fall greater, so Jason resolved to deal with and overcome his addiction alone.

This was unsuccessful. Eventually, his wife began to notice something different about him. Before they had married, Jason had told her about his occurrences of looking at porn, but he chalked it up to something guys typically experience a few times and said that it was over; no big deal. Back to the present: As she began to grow suspicious, she asked point-blank if he was looking at pornography.

Worn out, guilty, ashamed and tired of repenting only to relapse, Jason was finished with hiding the addiction. In utter brokenness and exhaustion, Jason answered yes. He was at the end of himself and did not want to hide his struggle in the shadows any longer. The inevitable consequence of losing his job did not matter any longer; Jason just wanted to be in the light, free from the bondage.

That next morning, Jason shared his struggle with his boss at the church. And as he confessed the sin he had struggled with for so many years, the chains began to break! It was the turning point in his life that he had been looking for.

Although Jason did lose his job, the church walked through the restoration process with him beautifully. His wife, appreciative of his honesty with her, walked through the season by his side as well. The two began professional counseling sponsored by the church, where Jason was able to address the root of his addiction.

In the restorative process, Jason began to realize that the heavy responsibilities of leadership and the false belief that a leader does not admit weakness fed his escape into pornography. But instead of needing an escape, Jason realized he needed to depend on a greater source of strength. He needed to be transparent and vulnerable in order to find the final conviction to do it in God's strength and not his. His untouchable belief began to shatter in the aftermath of his sin. No longer did he believe the addiction could be ignored or managed by his own ability; he knew he needed to confront it and find support to do so.

Out of his honesty and confession, Jason's life began to change! He started to see God's heart—that his Father desired authenticity, that Jason was meant to live in the light, not the shadows. And that out of an admission of weakness, he could be strengthened for a life free from addiction.

Jason points to 1 Peter 5:5–6 as a valuable lesson he learned on his journey: "'God opposes the proud but gives grace to the humble.' Humble yourselves, therefore, under the mighty hand of God so that at the proper time he may exalt you." Grace was never more apparent to Jason than it was at that point in his life. Up till then he thought he knew what was best for him; he tried to navigate his struggles on his own. But God resists the proud and those who think they have it figured out. When Jason submitted himself to God's work in his life, confessed his sin and admitted his weakness, out of that humility God extended an immense amount of grace, and Jason experienced freedom from bondage.

When Jason shared his story with me, he did so with wisdom forged in the fire of an epic fail and a hard season, but also out of incredible grace and redemption. He began to speak of the price Jesus paid on the cross for him and that the victory was won. He did not have to carry the burden alone and, furthermore, he knew that only Jesus could provide freedom from the bondage. No longer did Jason feel the need to try so hard to keep a lid on his struggle. He had learned that openness, communication and vulnerability are necessary.

He was eventually asked to join a church plant, where he now serves as a pastor. Two years after bringing his sin into the light, Jason shared his testimony at the church, which led to incredible opportunities to help others walk through hard seasons.

Jason no longer buys into the myth that he can be free from his weakness simply by thinking that he will never fall into it again. He knows the battle is not over, that he must never stop depending on Jesus lest he desire to escape into an addiction again. Having fallen as he did, Jason now realizes he is not strong enough to avoid sin by putting the possibility out of his mind. He knows he must guard against temptation. Jason attributes the healthy, vibrant life he now lives to accountability, the willingness to admit weakness and boundaries.

Jason shared eloquently with me that he did not fall from grace, but that he fell right into it.

Jason could not have imagined he would end up doing what he did. Just as I never imagined I would end up doing what I did. But both stories illustrate that buying into the untouchable myth gives one a false sense of security because it does not allow room to build in guardrails, only naïve "nevers." It is a false sense of safety to say, "I'll never"; it provides no bumpers for protection. Because I said, "I would never," I lived in a dream world far away from the reality of what could happen. It was there, in that alternate universe, that I failed to implement protective measures.

Do you have your own list of "nevers"? What is on that list? An affair, stealing from your employer, depending on a drug, a pornography addiction? Any of these and more are certainly possibilities in your life, just as sex outside of marriage was one for me. If you choose to ignore the possibility, you will forever live in a place where that sin could very much be something you do.

The untouchable myth starts with a lack of preparedness. Do you live there, on the very thin line between sureness and naïvety? This is the brink of an untouchable mindset.

Not only did my "I would never" mentality hurt me but so did my incomplete healing from sexual bondage. I lived in a world where I believed my past would not come back to haunt me or affect my new relationship. Sex was my bondage, and I was in a relationship with an attractive man—why I never put two and two together is beyond me. My only defense is the immense blindness I lived in under the untouchable myth.

What is a core issue you struggle with? Is there something from your past that you have buried deep within? Chances are, the unresolved issues will come back to bite you, especially in a new way, if not dealt with properly and guarded against. Perhaps you have learned to gain temporary victory over a stronghold and have tucked it away as "dealt with," as I had with sexual bondage.

Do not be so bold as to think that a past struggle could never be a struggle for you again. It is these very areas where you must be vigilant to guard yourself. Perhaps that means checking off something on your "never" list. The enemy will not give up and will certainly find new ways to get at your vulnerability.

Playing into Your Weakness

We all have weaknesses, whether we know it or not. The Bible tells us that Samson had one, but he refused to accept that he would ever succumb to it. He lived a life of grandeur, doing whatever he pleased. But let's start at the beginning of his story.

The book of Judges (chapters 13–16) tells us the story of a woman who had been barren for many years. The "angel of the Lord" appeared to her and told her she would conceive and bear a son, and also provided guidelines for her and the child. She was given one key rule: Never let a razor touch his head for he was to be a Nazirite, and he would begin the deliverance of Israel from the Philistines.

Samson was born and kept this one law for most of his life, although many of the Nazirite laws he did not. He married a Philistine woman and had sexual relations with a prostitute. He ate honey from a dead animal, which would have been considered unclean. I also cannot help but pick up a hint of disrespect for his parents and substantial pride. It is no secret, however, that his greatest weakness was women.

Regardless of Samson's struggles and failures, God had divinely chosen him and placed His favor on the Israelite. From what we read in the Bible, Samson killed 1,030 Philistines and slaughtered many more before they captured him. He made such a huge impact on their nation that the Philistines pursued him at every opportunity.

It was not until he gave in to his lust for a woman named Delilah that he was overpowered. Three separate times the temptress asked Samson to tell her the source of his great strength, and three times he lied. Three times the Philistines rushed in to capture Samson, and each time he prevailed over them.

You would think at this point that Samson would never tell Delilah his true source of strength, if not dump her altogether. But the fourth time she asked, he told her that his strength was in his hair (palm on forehead—am I right?). At that, she shaved off his hair when he was sleeping, and the Philistines overpowered him. The great Samson was taken prisoner, blinded and mocked. All because he failed to guard himself against his weakness for women.

Fortunately for Samson, God is a good Father and never gave up on the man (nor does He us). His hair began to grow back, and at a party with thousands of the most powerful Philistines in attendance, Samson prayed to God for strength one final time to bring the building down as a final blow to Israel's enemies. I am moved by his prayer because it is the most humble and God-focused prayer he uttered in his entire life. Having been stripped of everything—physical strength, freedom, sight, pleasure, pride—Samson finally found a (spiritual) strength he had always lacked. In his most humble state he gained the greatest victory.

As I read this account I cannot help but gather that Samson truly believed he was untouchable. He could not imagine that a woman could ever bring him down—the mighty Samson. He was the great warrior who had defeated many hundreds of Philistines; a woman was the least of his worries. He certainly did not fathom that his great source of strength would also become his greatest weakness. This denial led him down a path of destruction.

We see from his story that the untouchable myth will play into a preexisting weakness in three ways:

1. You may not realize that something is indeed a weakness.
2. Something becomes a weakness because you are not properly guarding against it.
3. Your strength may very well be a weakness.

To speak to the first point, I never fully realized that sex outside of marriage would be a weakness for me and something that I needed to guard against. I knew my past, but in my mind "I would never," so it did not seem to me to be a threat. I no longer perceived my past weakness as current weakness, which was a big mistake. It is like a recovering alcoholic thinking he can walk into a bar and stay sober simply because he has resolved never to drink again.

Perhaps you have a weakness brewing underneath the surface. You think you have dealt with it and never imagine that it could remain a current threat. You are denying the fact that, under just the right circumstances, it could very much lead to your fall.

Regarding the second point, it is possible that something you have never dealt with can become a weakness simply because you are not guarding against the fact that you are vulnerable to a variety of temptations. Most people have not set out to steal, cheat or deceive. Yet under the right circumstances I believe anyone is capable of doing anything. With just the right pressure, you could very well step into a sin that you never considered to be a threat. This is why it is important to guard yourself in all areas of life, but we will get to that in a later chapter.

And regarding the third point, an area of strength could easily become your weakness. Look at Samson. His strength made him feel invincible, yet it was his strength that attracted the enemy. Samson never perceived that the source of his strength, when targeted, would be his downfall. His strength was a vulnerable area, not insurance against weakness.

Perhaps you have always been a confident person, but you play with pride. Or perhaps you set high expectations for yourself, but your unspoken high expectations for others lead to confrontation and conflict. Or perhaps you have a tender heart toward people, but you allow others to influence your decisions as you struggle with peer pressure. Just be careful that where you thrive does not become a weakness and a place where you also become an unprepared target.

The Enemy Loves Fatigue

For most of us there is a knee-jerk reaction of confidence in our ability to be strong (much like Samson). Nobody loves admitting weakness. But are you thinking through all the possibilities?

What if you are tired, worn down and exhausted? It is hard to be strong against temptation when you are weary. I can look back at the time of my epic fail and see that, although it was a fun and fulfilling season, it was also draining. I was pushing to maintain a high level of ministry activities, including speaking and writing, and also was committed to building a relationship with Ryan.

Not that there is ever an okay reason to sin, but weariness was definitely a contributing factor for me. The enemy saw my vulnerability even when I could not see it. He saw my fatigue and a perfect opportunity to gain a foothold in my life.

Let's learn about this from the great prophet Elijah and his own season of weariness. In 1 Kings 19, we read that Elijah was reeling from the famous defeat of the Baal prophets on Mount Carmel. He had called down fire from heaven in front of all of Israel, and in one mighty blow he had crushed the people's faith in the false god, which led to national repentance. Instead of riding a wave of confidence, though, he fell into depression.

Elijah was worn out. So much so that he collapsed under a tree and wished to die. Elijah, the man whose prayers raised a dead child to life. The man who dared to ban rain from the land for three and a half years. The man who ran twenty miles ahead of a chariot in supernatural strength. This man was exhausted and done. Finished.

In his exhaustion, Elijah went through rough emotions and gave up. This can happen to us as well as we come off a mountain and hit the valley. No doubt the enemy, a roaring lion, senses our fatigue and a perfect opportunity to make a move on his prey. Having thoughts of suicide was not normal for Elijah; it was an attack as a result of his fatigue.

God, however, provided nourishment for Elijah to be strengthened and continue on. A forty-day journey later, Elijah had an incredible experience with God on Mount Horeb. But it was subtle. It was not in the wind, earthquake or fire that God revealed Himself to Elijah; it was in a gentle whisper. It was not in the obvious but in the intimate. God was tenderly speaking to His prophet on the heels of an epic high, followed by a dark and lonely low. It is a beautiful connection between the Father and His child. One you can experience for yourself.

There will be seasons in your life, perhaps, when you do not even fully realize that you are exhausted in some way—spiritually, physically, emotionally or mentally. Maybe in all four ways (coming from a working mom with a newborn, it is possible!). Don't be naïve: Fatigue leaves the door open to failure.

If you are worn down and tired, take some time for yourself. Shut the door, turn on some music and spend some valuable time with the Lord. Have your own intimate time with Him as Elijah did. Maybe go away for the weekend on a miniretreat without social media and distractions. Find a babysitter and go on a fun, romantic date with your spouse. Whatever rest might look like for you, make room for it. Be rejuvenated and get a bit of that strength back.

I share this because there will be seasons when you are tired, and you will leave a door open to weakness. Know now that it is possible. When you are worn out, the right pressure under the right circumstances makes frailty likely. Never dismiss weakness as inconsequential; realize that weakness can be either a door to failure or a place of intimacy with the Father. Will you choose intimacy?

How This Myth Affects You

The untouchable myth whispers lies to you. It deceives you. It tells you that you are invincible and far from moral failure. The wise person, however, considers the opposite; the wise ones take the words of Proverbs 22:3 seriously: "The prudent sees danger and hides himself, but the simple go on and suffer for it."

See the danger now because I am telling you that you are *not* untouchable. And to be frank, you are capable of any sin. Let that be your warning so that you no longer live in blindness, so that you no longer live as one who is "simple." Hide yourself from the danger of the untouchable myth; flee from it. Put as much distance between you and the myth as possible.

It is this myth, above all, that makes you vulnerable. It does this because unless you guard yourself intentionally, you are susceptible to failure. This myth is extremely dangerous. Without knowing the danger until it is too late, the mightiest fall. The myth lulls you into believing that you are safe, when in reality you are in danger and, eventually, your weakness will catch up with you.

Will you be prudent and hide yourself from the dangers of the untouchable myth, or will you ignore it and suffer down the road?

---------------------| GOING DEEPER |---------------------

1. Is there a strength you possess that could lead to a great weakness, like the example of confidence leading to pride? What area could that be? How might you be able to grow in a way that maintains the strength?

2. Seasons of weariness are normal; we all have them. If you are fatigued, what can you do to find rest in your current season? What would rejuvenation look like to you today?

CLOSING PRAYER

God, You are my strength. Rest isn't always easy to find, but when my body and soul need rejuvenation, I pray I will find it in Your presence. Please help me to stand firm against the enemy's schemes. I lean on You in my exhaustion. When I'm in this place, and indeed at all times, help me to be strong in You. I also pray that no matter the season, You would equip me to be prepared. You have given me certain strengths; help me to thrive there rather than get entangled by them. You are my victory, and in You I put my trust. Amen.

Part 2

THE TRUTH ABOUT THE MYTH

4

The Rooster Crows

Jesus said to him, "Truly, I tell you, this very night, before the rooster crows, you will deny me three times." Peter said to him, "Even if I must die with you, I will not deny you!" And all the disciples said the same.

Matthew 26:34–35

Simon was an ordinary man; a fisherman on the Sea of Galilee. He had a family, some friends, a job and a wife. There was nothing outwardly extraordinary about him. He was not an eloquent preacher in the area or a man of popularity. Nothing that would seem to qualify him as a disciple, apostle or pillar of the early Church. Truth is, he was living what we would consider a pretty ordinary life until one eventful day—when the Son of God showed up on the scene.

One day Andrew, Simon's brother, came to Simon to tell him he had found the Messiah! Naturally Simon went to see this Messiah—Jesus—and they met for the first time. It was there that Jesus renamed Simon as *Peter*, meaning "rock" or "stone." It seems a bit odd that Jesus would rename a person He was meeting for the first time; imagine being Simon Peter in that moment! It was, however, an important moment for the fisherman. This new name would be indicative of the role Peter would one day play in the early Church.

In his book *Twelve Ordinary Men* (Nelson, 2002), John MacArthur writes this about Peter:

> Jesus changed Simon's name, it appears, because He wanted the nickname to be a perpetual reminder to him about who he should be. And from that point on, whatever Jesus called him sent a subtle message. If He called him Simon, He was signaling him that he was acting like his old self. If He called him Rock, He was commending him for acting the way he ought to be acting.

Peter did not seem to be equipped for his official calling; not quite yet. But the potential was there and Jesus saw it. We get glimpses of that moment in Matthew, Mark and Luke. In these accounts Jesus called Peter to be a fisher of men, and it was then that Peter left behind everyone and everything—he gave up the ordinary life he had always known for an extraordinary journey of faith following Jesus. A life filled with both trials and miracles. His life was taking a dramatic turn.

Peter the Disciple

Peter embarked on an incredible journey with eleven other ordinary men as the disciples of Jesus, men devoted to following the Son of God. Peter was the kind of person who would ask questions the rest were thinking and speak up to offer his opinion on the matter (although it was not always thought out well). His personality was interesting—bold, impulsive, loyal, brave, legalistic and venturing into faith but with second thoughts. Reminds me a little of myself!

Peter was often the first to dive into a venture or step out in faith, but he was also often the first one out. His eagerness was admirable, but his lack of commitment to see it through left something to be desired.

Peter was the disciple who walked on water out to Jesus during the storm but began to fear and sink. In an incredible example of faith, he proclaimed that Jesus was the Son of God yet later was rebuked by Jesus for denying He would die. Peter was part of Jesus' inner circle, present as He prayed in the Garden of Gethsemane the night of His arrest. Yet that same night, impulsive Peter drew a sword and cut off the ear of the high priest's servant.

Peter had his strengths and weaknesses, as we all do. Yet Jesus, knowing everything about Peter, still chose to bring him into the inner circle and use him to help build the early Church. I love that God, knowing every weakness and hidden thought, still chooses to call us, use us and love us just as He did Peter.

The One Who "Would Never"

I bring Peter up because his story in the hours leading up to Jesus' death represents the untouchable myth perhaps better than any other story in the Bible. It all began after the famous Last Supper. Jesus had brought His disciples to the Mount of Olives under the dark canopy of night. It was there Jesus told the disciples they would soon scatter as it was written: "Strike the shepherd, and the sheep will be scattered" (Zechariah 13:7).

Peter was the first to proclaim he would never fall away; he would never "scatter." Even when Jesus told Peter that he would deny Him three times before the rooster crowed, Peter declared, "Even if I must die with You, I will not deny You."

"Deny Jesus" was solid on Peter's list of "I would never." He was so sure he would never abandon Jesus that he did not even make room for the possibility that it could happen. You would think by now Peter would have a pretty good grasp of Jesus' insight and would trust that anything Jesus prophesied would actually happen. But instead of accepting the truth of what Jesus said, Peter denied it emphatically.

Peter could have received what Jesus said and prepared himself. But he chose not to. In fact, it was right after warning him that Jesus brought Peter into the garden with two other disciples. He asked the three men to keep watch and pray while Jesus Himself prayed out of great sorrow and heaviness regarding what was to come.

While Jesus was apart from them, praying that the cup might pass, Peter and the other two disciples fell asleep. When Jesus returned and found them sleeping, He called them out. Specifically, He called out Simon. Not Peter, but Simon. Jesus was speaking to that old self because Peter had fallen into weakness. "Simon, are you asleep? Could you not watch one hour? Watch and pray that you may not enter into temptation. The spirit indeed is willing, but the flesh is weak" (Mark 14:37–38).

Jesus returned to prayer, and two more times He came back to find Peter sleeping. Here is how it could have gone differently. Peter could have regarded what Jesus had said earlier about the coming denial. He could have then used the few valuable moments he had in the garden to pray. Jesus gave clear warning that Peter was in a moment when the flesh was weak, so I am surprised that Peter did not jump to prayer after being called out the first time. But then again, am I really? Because I know I have fallen asleep spiritually just before the harder seasons of my life. My story of moral failure earlier in this book is one example.

I think this does serve as a warning to you and me, though. A caution always to be alert, especially when we are most tired or complacent. The enemy catches us best when we are tired (spiritually or physically) and when we set ourselves on cruise control because all is well. Yet we are called to be on guard at all times and, furthermore, to "pray without ceasing" (1 Thessalonians 5:17).

I cannot help but imagine that if Peter had taken Jesus' words to heart and been fervent in prayer in the garden, what happened next could have looked very different. But instead, what happened next was action birthed out of the untouchable myth.

It began after the arrest of Jesus, when the Son of God was led to the high priest for questioning. In Mark 14 we read that Peter followed behind to see what was happening. He did not venture too close or get involved; he remained just far enough behind to see what was going on without being caught in the middle of the injustice being done to Jesus. He was both curious and afraid at the same time.

Mark 14:54 tells us that "Peter had followed him at a distance, right into the courtyard of the high priest. And he was sitting with the guards and warming himself at the fire." This might not seem like a big deal; in fact, some might comment that at least Peter was following Jesus. But in truth, it is not the loveliest account of Peter. You see, Peter was sitting by the fire with the guards instead of staying close to Jesus. The guards would eventually lead Jesus to the cross and see to His death—this was the kind of company Peter was in. If Peter had truly trusted

Jesus, he would have remained by His side as long as possible, knowing that Jesus could protect him. Nothing could happen to Peter that was not in Jesus' plan. Yet he kept at a distance that allowed him to remain uninvolved and away from danger, even if that cost him closeness to Jesus.

Peter has shown us thus far that we fail to live up to the righteousness we are called to *when we deny the possibility of failure, coast on complacency and keep ourselves at a distance from Jesus in order to protect some part of ourselves.* The pinnacle of Peter's failure, however, came when he denied Jesus.

Peter's Untouchable Myth Busted

Peter did the very thing he said he would never do: He denied Jesus—three times. *Three times.* What is fascinating to me is that he did not even realize he was doing it, even after being warned hours before, until it was too late. In the midst of his failure, he had no idea he was doing the very thing he said he would never do.

Let's get a better idea of what this looked like. Matthew 26:69–75 gives a clear description.

As Peter was sitting in the courtyard with the guards, a girl recognized him and identified him as someone who followed Jesus. *Peter denied it* and left. Another girl saw him and called him out as well, and that time *Peter declared with an oath* that it was not true. Finally, bystanders pointed Peter out, and that time *Peter invoked a curse and swore* he did not know Jesus.

This progression shows deepening disillusionment from Peter's untouchable mentality. He began by simply denying he knew Jesus, then promised with an oath that he was speaking the truth and ended with a curse and swearing. Only when the rooster crowed did he realize his failure: He had done what Jesus said he would do.

Denial can be blinding. If Peter could deny Jesus just hours after being warned he would, and if he never realized it was happening until after the fact, then you can also be blind to sin in the middle of the act. This is why wising up to the untouchable myth and preparing yourself for what lies ahead are vital for standing firm when temptation comes. Without this acceptance, denial will blind you until after the fact, just as it did Peter.

Peter proves to us that there is an untouchable mentality out there and that it can happen to anyone. Peter was one of the twelve disciples and one of the closest to Jesus, yet even he fell into this trap. If he could fail, how can we say that we would not, or that our pastor, friend or spouse could not do the same? Peter shows us that we are all vulnerable to the untouchable myth when we are unwilling to admit our weakness(es).

If Peter had heeded Jesus' warning, guarded himself properly with prayer and stayed close to Jesus, imagine how differently this story could have turned out for him. Perhaps he never would have denied Jesus at all and, instead of cowering in shame, could have stood there faithfully by his Lord in those final moments. We will never know how his story could have looked different, but there is certainly the possibility that it could have had a better ending.

Prayer and Proximity

Besides admitting weakness, which we will discuss more in a later chapter, let's look more closely at the two things Peter could have done differently: prayed (instead of coasting along on complacency) and maintained proximity (instead of remaining at a distance).

Prayer is a powerful tool; dare I say it is one of the most powerful tools we have as Christians? When utilized it can be effective in preparing us for and winning the battle. Our youth pastor, Scotty Gibbons, used to tell us often that "the battle is won in prayer." I did not grasp the magnitude of this statement in my youth, but I understand it now. God responds to, moves through and delights in the prayers of His people. Without that communion with God, we miss out on great intimacy with Him. Furthermore, prayer activates power in our battles. I can tell you from experience that I would rather fight a battle on my knees than on my feet and in my own strength. Can I get an *Amen*?

Yes, Peter was tired, I am sure. I know how hard it is to keep those eyes open as they grow heavier and heavier (no matter how good the movie is). But the heaviness of the moment and what was about to happen should have been a motivator for Peter to pray. He was not perfect and neither are we, but we need to learn from his experience.

When you are tired, frustrated, weak or complacent, are you likely to pray harder and more often? If you are anything like me, probably not. But we can learn from Peter and our own past failures to become people who pray, people who go into battle with prayer.

Is this something you want to embrace for your own life? To have a track record of dropping to your knees in surrender and praying to the Father with vigor and tenacity? To be like the persistent widow who came to the judge over and over again, undaunted, to have her request granted? Will people recall, as they reflect on your life one day, that you were a person of prayer?

Nothing has driven me to prayer like being a mama has. I have a precious newborn son, and I yearn for him to have a mom he knows prays. I long for him one day to remember fondly all the times he saw his mother surrendered in prayer. That is the memory I want him to have of me perhaps more than anything. And I pray it is a habit he embraces at a young age.

What kind of life—of legacy—do you want to have? One with prayer or one without? I can tell you that with prayer you will be able to look back and see God's work in and through your life in a powerful way that would not be possible without prayer.

I guarantee Peter wished he had prayed in those moments in the garden instead of sleeping.

Peter also could have done better with proximity that night. I imagine he longed to be right there next to Jesus in the Messiah's final hours. His proximity was not where it could have been. Peter distanced himself from Jesus and ended up spending a short period of time with the very people who would lead the Savior to His death.

Where is your proximity today? Are you sticking close to Jesus no matter what people might think or say? Regardless of the persecution or mockery, are you staying connected to the vine? Or are you keeping yourself at a safe distance so your co-workers or friends will not judge you for your faith?

Do you want to see Jesus only from afar? To know He is there but not be close enough to have any real intimacy with Him? Or do you want to be right there with Him, in partnership with the Savior?

Intimacy with Jesus is one of the sweetest things on this earth. Never let fear of what others think rob you of such a gift. You hold the decision in your hands for the kind of relationship you have with Him. You determine how close you and your Savior can be.

Peter's Redemption

When I read Peter's story about those final hours with Jesus, I cannot help but see myself. We both had an untouchable mentality, and that myth cost us both something dear. What we lost in those moments can never be regained, no matter how much we regret our actions or try to make up for the wrong. Perhaps you see yourself in his story as well. Many of us can bear witness to the sadness of such a story; we know the regret and shame that follow an epic fail. For those who cannot relate, there is still time for you! Time to embrace weakness, prayer and proximity.

What is encouraging about Peter's story is that it did not end there. He made a mistake, but Jesus did not cast him to the side for his failure. Instead Jesus reinstated him (see John 21:15–19). After the death of Jesus, Peter retreated to what he knew—fishing. He was out on the water with some of the other disciples when Jesus appeared on the shore. Peter was so overcome with eagerness he threw himself into the sea and swam to Jesus, where the two men would engage in intimate conversation, one that would bring healing to Peter's guilt-ridden heart. Peter was able to forgive himself and move forward. He did indeed become the rock that Jesus named him to be.

The Bible shows us that after the resurrection, Peter would exhibit leadership among the apostles, preach the first sermon at Pentecost, be influential in the early Church and reach out to Gentiles with the Gospel.

If Peter—who was brash, impetuous and quick to make empty promises—could fall into an untouchable mindset, fumble so greatly and see God redeem him for a great purpose, there is hope for you and me! His story shows us that while the myth does exist, we do not have to live with it forever.

Not that our epic fails are okay, but they can definitely add value to our callings if we allow God to shape us through them. Peter had his ups and downs, and those final hours with Jesus were the hardest he probably faced, but coming out of that experience, he was shaped into a better follower of Christ and better leader for the early Church. Jesus knew what Peter had in him. Yes, he was Simon who could make reckless mistakes, but he was also Peter, a strong and dependable rock.

Forged in his trials to be less like Simon, Peter went on to do great things in the name of Jesus. He allowed his epic fail to shape him for good. Will you take the same challenge? Will you allow your past failures and mistakes to shape you into a more committed follower of Christ? Never use sin as an excuse for transformation, but do allow your failures to forge a better you.

There is hope—hope anchored in Jesus who redeems and restores! Just be willing to admit weakness is possible, be fervent in prayer and stay in close proximity to Jesus.

GOING DEEPER

1. How is your prayer life? Are you struggling like Peter to make it a priority, or is it vibrant? If you are struggling, recommit to making it important to you. Decide how you might be able to follow through in this decision, whether that be scheduling a time in your calendar each day or removing tasks that might be unnecessary to your life.

2. How is your proximity? Is it your desire to grow closer to Him each day, or are you drifting further from Him? If you are drifting, find ways to build in time with Him

when you can focus on your intimacy. How might this look? Are there things in your life you need to remove in order to grow closer to Him? Determine what needs to go and what needs to be added in order to draw near to God.

———————————| CLOSING PRAYER |———————————

Lord, I long to be as close to You as I can. May I learn from Peter's story. Show me how I can grow as a result of diving into what he went through. Help me to grow into a prayer warrior and be someone who is always right at Your feet. Prayer and proximity are deeply important to me. Intimacy with You is my greatest desire. I love You, God. To You be the glory. Amen.

5

Living in Denial

If we say we have no sin, we deceive ourselves, and the truth is not in us.

1 John 1:8

As I write this, it has been three weeks since I gave birth to my handsome son, Roman. He is our first child, and the whole experience of pregnancy, labor and recovery has been completely new to me. I had no idea what to expect on this journey, in all honesty, as much as I prepared myself to be prepared!

In pregnancy I developed the dreaded gestational diabetes and a severe case of PUPPP (a rash all over the body that itches like crazy); both were hard and at times straight up miserable. Those last few weeks, as the summer picked up, all I could do each night after work was crash on the couch, put my feet in a bowl of ice water, place a fan right in front of me and binge watch Netflix. It wasn't always the pregnancy I had hoped for, but I could roll with that if it meant getting this beautiful child at the end of the journey. In addition, besides not getting the natural labor I had hoped for and an epidural gone wrong the first time (which was painful!), labor was doable as well, and I made it through (despite the first-time parent jitters).

Once I had Roman, I thought I was in the clear. I did not get the easy pregnancy or fault-free natural labor I had hoped and planned for, but I was okay with that. And once Roman was here, I thought I was all set to go home and settle into a new normal with my growing family. I thought the disappointment and difficulty were behind me.

A few hours before I was discharged from the hospital, I began to feel nauseous and weak. In fact, after I was officially discharged, I had to take a nap in the hospital bed before I left just to make it home alert. I was told and was sure that it was the result of not getting more than five hours of sleep in three days, so it did not seem like a big deal at the time.

When I arrived home with my handsome husband and precious son, I was soon wiped out again and lay down for a three-hour nap. I felt guilty needing the sleep, but I was truly nauseous and was given assurance that I needed sleep in order to take care of my son well.

When I woke up, I did feel better and enjoyed the evening with my family. That night at nine, however, I began to experience severe cramping. Within thirty minutes my pain level went from a two to a seven, and I knew something was not right; I told Ryan I needed to go to the ER. With tears welling in my eyes, I looked right into the big blue eyes of my newborn son and told him good-bye as I left him for the first time, so suddenly, with my parents. It was one of the most heart-wrenching moments of my life, to leave him so soon. Already the guilt began to set in.

After more than five hours in the emergency room, undergoing tests and trying multiple pain medications to find one that would work, I was finally admitted to the intensive care unit in the middle of the night for a rare ovarian blood clot. Ryan and I were exhausted as they shut off the lights in my small hospital room at four that Monday morning.

I spent three days in the ICU instead of at home with my newborn son. My heart yearned for his little self. To see him look up at me with those gorgeous blue eyes I had come to adore and wrap his little hand around my finger. Thankfully, we were finally able to bring him into the room with us for the remainder of the stay, but it is not ideal to start a journey as a family in the ICU. I could no longer roll with the punches, and I began to break down.

The emotional toll of being in the ICU, having a painful blood clot and being away from Roman began to overwhelm me. If you are a parent, you understand the difficulty of leaving your child for the first time; imagine doing it so soon. It was in that hospital room that the enemy began to whisper words of shame and guilt over me. He began to tell me that I was a failure, that I was letting down my husband as a wife and my son as a mom. The thoughts were only enhanced when I discovered I could no longer breastfeed due to the blood thinners I would be on for several months. The condemnation was overwhelming, and I felt like a failure more than ever before. I was letting down the people I cared about most in one of the most significant seasons of my life. That hospital stay and first few days at home were one of the most emotional times in my life.

Why am I sharing this painful season with you? Because I had expectations and a plan for how my pregnancy, labor and postdelivery would look. I never considered the possibility, although I knew it existed, that I would not be able to breastfeed. I certainly never imagined being apart from my son so soon. But when those things happened—when my plan and expectations were not met—I fell into incredible discouragement.

I was in denial that anything could go wrong; I wanted to believe that the whole experience would go exactly how I had prepared and hoped it would. I should have been open to the possibility that my pregnancy and labor might not go as planned. As I mentioned earlier, I was able to roll with the punches in those early phases, but I reached a breaking point in that small hospital room. The denial I had lived in for months now weighed on my emotional heart, and I collapsed under the pressure.

Here is the truth: Life never goes as planned. We can prepare, set the table and make all the arrangements for a life we have envisioned, but God always sees a bigger picture that we cannot see. You and I cannot foresee the future or avoid the bumps along the journey. We simply navigate them with Christ-centered focus and have faith in the God who does see the bigger picture.

Reality is, there will be times in your life when you feel disappointed. Yet in those moments, you have an anchor for your soul. Although you might feel caught in the turbulent waves, Christ is your guiding light in the storm. And though you might be a bit disoriented, all is well with your soul when He is in control.

There is a worship song that helped carry me through my postbaby emotional roller coaster. It lived on repeat during those weeks. And now, it is the song I sing and gently rock my son to sleep to every night. The words from "It Is Well" by Bethel Music were a constant reminder to me that my soul was well, even though the circumstances seemed unsure and difficult, because my eternity was settled. No matter what, God is good, He is in control and one day I will get to experience incredible joy with Him in heaven. No circumstances can change that.

Living in denial hurts us all because life is unpredictable. I was in denial when I believed everything would go as planned. Because I did not make room for the possibility that things could go differently from what I desired, the discouragement was heavier and was felt more significantly.

We can be thankful that our souls have an anchor. A God who steadies us in the waves and the wind. A calm force in the storm.

Denial Hurts

Denial is blinding. It keeps you from a realistic perspective and, thus, holds you in a world where the untouchables can never affect you. In this world, preparation is not a priority. Failure is not an option. Messy is not a possibility.

I generally live life with rose-colored glasses; believing that good prevails and the best can happen. Remember in chapter 1 when I mentioned the birth of my optimism and how it lent itself to my untouchable mentality? To be clear, optimism is not a bad thing. In fact, I believe it is a very good thing. Optimism speaks the language of hope and faith. It looks at a dire situation and sees opportunity for something better. Optimism is a beautiful gift in a dark world that shines a light to illuminate the good.

Optimism, however, can also contribute to blindness or naïvety. It can diminish a realistic big picture by focusing on pockets of good and, thus, blind us to the potential for harm.

This was the case for me when I was in my early twenties. I allowed my unwavering optimism to negate the possibility that any untouchables could affect me. I went through life with blinders on those rose-colored glasses. I missed the pitfalls to my right and left; I saw only the beautiful scene I had painted down the road.

Truth is, I was living in a world of pretend. Like the little girl envisioning herself as the fair princess picking flowers and talking to the animals on a warm and sunny day. I was pretending failure was not an option. Pretending that my past weakness was not a weakness anymore. Pretending that everything would work out how I wanted it to just because I said it would.

What about you? Are you deceived by believing that nothing can go wrong? That your world will progress as planned? That everything is going to be perfect? Or are you willing to step into the truth that anything is possible? Denial or truth—only one can exist in your belief system.

A pretend world involves acting. Acting as though nothing bad will happen and that you are invincible. But the role an actor plays is not lived in the real world, is it? No. It lives in an imaginary world, and when you pretend that you are untouchable, you are not living in a realistic world either. You are an actor playing pretend.

Acting is not rooted in the real world, and it is not rooted in truth. As a believer, you are called to pursue truth. To be aware and knowledgeable. This means you must refrain from living in the unrealistic world of denial. Be open to the possibility that anything is possible. This is a truth that can set you free.

The Fear Factor

To be honest about my living in an unreal world with an untouchable mindset, I have to say that I gave center stage to one of the key causes of denial: fear. Fear is one of the most powerful emotions we can experience as human beings and, sadly, one of the easiest to let run our lives.

Some people just flat out choose denial because of fear. Fear that if they acknowledge any possibility of failure, they are more likely to fail. Fear that if they admit weakness they will never be able to hide it from others. Or fear of facing something ugly inside themselves. Fear is dictating their approaches to life, and many find living in denial to be, well, easier.

Fear will always be a hindrance to your life if you allow it to sit in the driver's seat. It takes over the life you are meant to live. When you allow fear to direct your thoughts, you are allowing something to hinder the fullness you are meant to experience. It paralyzes you, immobilizes you.

If you are living in fear today and find even the smallest evidence that it is perpetuating an untouchable mindset, face your past and the fears you have pushed back into the corners of your soul, so that you can be an overcomer by the power of Christ! You do not have to live there; nor is it what God has for you, so commit to a new way of life here and now.

Fear distorts your perspective. It produces a false sense of security. It leads to desires for things that probably will not fulfill you. Mark 4:19 explains that false security and desires for the things of this world will choke out the Word and leave your life unfruitful. Is that the kind of life you want to live? Probably not. So let's take a look at how you can begin to overcome fear.

Overcoming a Mindset of Fear

I have found five principles that really help in overcoming fear:

1. A proper perspective
2. Trusting God to sustain you

3. A healthy fear of God

4. The cure for anxiety

5. Prayer and thanksgiving

If you have *a proper perspective*, denial is harder to achieve. Matthew 6:33 is one of my favorite verses in the Bible: "Seek first the kingdom of God and his righteousness, and all these things will be added to you." Jesus is illustrating that we humans worry about many things in our lives—worry that overflows from our fears. In response, He makes our mission in life clear: Put God first, and everything that we worry about will take care of itself.

Now, I get it—worry and fear come easily and can be hard to fight. But worry can also cause a great deal of damage to your ability to live out the plans God has for you. It seeps into your relationships, job and finances, to name just a few things. And when it gets in there, distrust and lack of faith take root.

Instead of having this distorted perspective, have a proper one. The proper direction for your eyes is not on the things of this world and your worries, but on God. When that perspective begins to get distorted, recite Matthew 6:33 and fix your eyes on Jesus. That might mean putting on some worship music or hitting the ground in prayer or stepping back from a situation.

If you can get your eyes on God and focus on Him, all those other elements will fall into place. You can cast your cares upon God, and God will take care of everything else. This is a vital first step in your journey.

Another key to overcoming fear is *trusting God to sustain you*. Have you ever wondered how you were going to get through a season or situation—especially when fear began to set in and play all sorts of mind games? Me, too. In fact, if I am completely transparent with you, I have been known to catastrophize. Which means I have a tendency to believe the worst may happen in a particularly hard situation. I know; contradicts my optimism, but somehow the two coexist!

Maybe you can relate? Maybe your mind wanders to the worst that can happen? We all struggle at times with a distorted perspective.

Isaiah 41:10 speaks to this place of fear: "Fear not, for I am with you; be not dismayed, for I am your God; I will strengthen you, I will help you, I will uphold you with my righteous right hand."

When you are fearful or dismayed, remind yourself of what God says in this verse—that He will strengthen you, help you and uphold you. The God who controls all things will be there to protect and aid you in your fear.

To add to that, Psalm 55:22 encourages you to cast your burden on Him. You are encouraged to do this because He can handle it; God can handle anything you give Him. Your worries, fears, shame, doubt—none of it is too much for Him to bear.

When you do cast it all on Him, He will sustain you. God wants you to know that you can lean on Him. That He will take care of you in the darkest of seasons. Will you let Him sustain you? Or will you carry it all alone?

In addition to trusting Him to sustain you, it is important to have a *healthy fear of God*. One way to overcome fear is to place a healthy fear in the proper place.

Just so you know, there is no one like God. In fact, there is no one who even comes close! How can you look at your situation—your fear—and size it up against our almighty God? You cannot. Fear trembles and caves in the shadow of our mighty and powerful God. Take that worry and look at it in contrast to His mightiness; you will probably start to get a better perspective.

Having a healthy fear of God—taking into account His mightiness, strength and ability to overcome anything—is a good thing. This does not mean labeling Him as unjust or angry and, therefore, someone to be feared; it means taking into account His character, realizing there is no one else like Him and believing that He can overcome what you fear.

When fear begins to creep in, remind yourself of who God really is and what He is capable of. That should help redirect your fear. It's a state of worship.

A close companion to fear is anxiety, and the Bible gives us a great *cure for anxiety*.

We are all looking for a cure for our ailments, are we not? We are looking for that "thing" that will bring instant relief to our anxiety or get us out of the difficult season. Cures are hard to come by, but we do find one for anxiety in Luke 12:22–34:

> And he said to his disciples, "Therefore I tell you, do not be anxious about your life, what you will eat, nor about your body, what you will put on. For life is more than food, and the body more than clothing. Consider the ravens: they neither sow nor reap, they have neither storehouse nor barn, and yet God feeds them. Of how much more value are you than the birds! And which of you by being anxious can add a single hour to his span of life? If then you are not able to do as small a thing as that, why are you anxious about the rest? Consider the lilies, how they grow: they neither toil nor spin, yet I tell you, even Solomon in all his glory was not arrayed like one of these. But if God so clothes the grass, which is alive in the field today, and tomorrow is thrown into the oven, how much more will he clothe you,

O you of little faith! And do not seek what you are to eat and what you are to drink, nor be worried. For all the nations of the world seek after these things, and your Father knows that you need them. Instead, seek his kingdom, and these things will be added to you.

"Fear not, little flock, for it is your Father's good pleasure to give you the kingdom. Sell your possessions, and give to the needy. Provide yourselves with moneybags that do not grow old, with a treasure in the heavens that does not fail, where no thief approaches and no moth destroys. For where your treasure is, there will your heart be also."

In this passage, Jesus is talking with His disciples about the topic of anxiety. He makes reference to the birds and the grass—God takes care of them. And if God takes care of them, how much more will He take care of you!

Worry and anxiety do not add any value to your day. In fact, they rob today of its value. Jesus says that He knows what you need. Indeed, pray for what you need, but never let the worry of what might happen drive you to a place of denial. Fix your eyes on the Father, and He will take care of all of these things.

So, what is the cure exactly?

1. *Remember that God already has your needs in mind (see Luke 12:30).* He knows what you really need in this life to thrive in the calling He has placed on your life. He knows your struggles and tension, even before you do. Nothing in your life will ever surprise Him, so trust Him to work all things out for good. Trust that He will take care of all your needs.

2. *Set your focus on Him (see verse 31).* Fix your eyes firmly on Him. Not on your needs or the fear but on Him. Look

only to Him in your hour of trouble. With this kind of focus, fears on the horizon disappear.

3. *Store up your treasures in heaven (see verse 33).* Live with a Kingdom purpose. This means living out your purpose with conviction, serving others, having pure motives and doing all things with the mission of building the Kingdom of God. May all that you do have eternal value.

If you can begin to implement these steps, you are on a path to victory over fear!

Finally, a key factor in overcoming fear is *prayer and thanksgiving*. In Philippians 4:6, we are called not to be anxious but to access God with our requests through prayer and thanksgiving.

If you are feeling any amount of anxiety, train yourself to turn to praise. Praise will shift your perspective and turn your heart in a healthy direction. How can fear thrive in an environment of praise? It cannot!

Watch that you are not led astray by denial and the fear that drives it—they are a hindrance to the enjoyment of life. It is hard to fight this natural tendency, but if you want to throw off the shackles of fear and stop living in denial, then fight that tendency with what you have learned in this chapter. Anything worth having (freedom) is worth fighting for.

Take the distorted perspective fear thrives in, and set your eyes on Jesus—the right perspective. Remember that God will sustain you in your difficult season or situation. Size up your concern next to the mightiness of our God, and see how it shudders in the shadow of His power. Then follow the cure outlined in Luke 12, and turn to praise and thanksgiving.

You can be set free from fear and denial, now that you have the tools to overcome them. Go to the throne and lean into the Father. He is with you in every battle!

GOING DEEPER

1. Are you living with any sort of fear? If so, what are you fearful of? Losing a job? Losing someone in your family? Perhaps not being able to support that family? Whatever your fear may be, commit to start confronting it instead of living in denial.

2. Which of the five ways to overcome fear spoke most to you? Which do you think might be an area you struggle with most? How can you start taking steps to implement into your life a plan to overcome your fear?

CLOSING PRAYER

O Father, I no longer want to live under the weight of fear. It is unhealthy and takes my focus off You. When fear begins to tighten on my heart and consume me, remind me to direct my gaze on You. I confess now that I have failed at this in the past and ask for forgiveness. But today is a new day, and I resolve to place my fear next to Your mightiness so that I might see how it shudders in light of Your authority. No longer will I live in denial; I lean into You. Amen.

6

A Hindrance

Lay aside every weight, and sin which clings so closely, and let us run with endurance the race that is set before us.

Hebrews 12:1

Having an untouchable mentality is a hindrance. It is a hindrance in the pursuit of God's call on your life, creating a barrier between where you are and where you could be. With this limited mindset and the vulnerability to sin, your trajectory is limited as well. This mindset is a denial, right? And denial does not live in the full truth and knowledge we are called to live in as believers.

Are you okay with living in a world where you are hindered from being all that God has created you to be? Where you are shackled to limitations and bounded by hopelessness? Probably not. Knowing that the untouchable mindset is a hindrance, are you prepared to spend your life as a runner facing obstacles? The track runner facing hurdles is constantly dodging a fall and at some point, if given enough time, will indeed fall.

The endurance runner, on the other hand, is faced only with the decision to keep running. We have a long race ahead of us; would you rather run it with hurdles or without? Either will be tiresome, but at least one route frees us from exerting extra energy.

As we run this race of endurance, Hebrews 12:1 directs us further to "lay aside every weight, and sin which clings so closely." You are called to live a life free from entanglement and limitation; free from weights that can cause you to fall in the race you are running. All sin is a hindering weight. Even things in your life that are good in moderation or in a certain context can become a hindering weight. Satan is just waiting for you to stumble.

Do you want to live life constantly jumping the hurdles of false security, burdened by extra weight, or would you rather run with endurance, free from the sin that clings closely? First Corinthians 9:24 encourages the believer with these words: "Do you not know that in a race all the runners run, but only one receives the prize? So run that you may obtain it."

Are you running your race—living this life—as if there is one prize to be obtained? Honestly, I am deeply convicted at this moment by this verse because I cannot say I always do. I have been known to get distracted and allow a few weights to hinder my race. But I do not want that for myself or for you. I want to encourage you to throw off the untouchable mindset and run this race as if only one person will win. If only I could be your daily cheerleader, encouraging you to run this race with everything you have!

At the end of your life would you like to hear, "Well done, good and faithful servant," upon your arrival before God? I know I would! May this thought ever be on your mind, constantly pushing you to live your life with purpose and purity, free from any hindrances.

Five Hindrances of the Untouchable Mindset

We saw in the last chapter how having an untouchable mindset means living in denial, and that denial hurts. When you live in denial, you make yourself vulnerable to everything on your untouchable list. You refuse to acknowledge reality and never prepare yourself to combat the temptations and trials that will come your way. You set up barriers and pick up weights that hinder you in the race set before you.

Through my own experience and after reading Peter's story in Matthew 26, I have identified five ways the untouchable mindset hinders us on our journeys:

1. Provides a false sense of security, leading you to believe you are invincible
2. Creates blinders to the reality around you
3. Distracts you from the spiritual disciplines
4. Does not allow you to be open to possibilities
5. Causes you to miss what God has in store for you

Provides a false sense of security, leading you to believe you are invincible. Do you have a list of sins you firmly believe you will never do? Your "of course, I will never do this" list? Without guardrails in place, you are vulnerable. Believing you are untouchable leads to believing you are invincible, at least in certain areas. This then gives a false sense of security.

Truth bomb: You are not invincible. No one is except God, and only He can say with certainty that He will not stumble. To believe otherwise is pride.

Remember the verse Jason shared as a valuable lesson he learned on his journey? First Peter 5:5–6 says this: "'God opposes the proud but gives grace to the humble.' Humble yourselves, therefore, under the mighty hand of God so that at the proper time he may exalt you." Pride is one of those things that God just does not stand for. Furthermore, it is a major hindrance in pursuing the call on your life. When you try to operate out of your own strength and abilities, you are operating out of pride. False security and an invincibility complex are prideful.

Proverbs 16:18 tells us that pride goes before a fall. I have witnessed this in my life and in so many others' lives. Pride must be humbled, and usually that happens with a mighty fall. Humbling yourself now by realizing you are not untouchable could spare you unnecessary pain.

If you go through life confident in your ability to be strong and stand firm against the devil's schemes, without any real protection, you are walking a dangerous path filled with obstacles. You might not be able to acknowledge that you have a false sense of security, but anyone with the untouchable mindset does indeed struggle with this at some level. I know in hindsight that in the back of my mind I believed I was strong enough to face anything. That I was untouchable. But we know how that ended.

Furthermore, when we have a false sense of security, we often believe we can go anywhere and try anything we want. Believing we are untouchable basically opens the door to doing whatever we want without consequence.

When I was 23 years old I spent the summer in Wyoming; it was a much-needed break from ministry and a spiritual retreat to refocus. I came out of that summer feeling pretty strong because I had spent four months with more than a hundred unbelievers in their twenties, and I had not fallen into the worldly activity buzzing all around me. I was on a spiritual high!

After that summer I was not entirely sure what God had next for me. I decided to return to Missouri to help with the upcoming women's conference I had been part of in the past. I hoped that God would show me where to go next during that time (in fact, I assumed He would because He had been with me so powerfully that summer).

At the time my family lived in Rhode Island, so in Missouri I lacked a place to stay long term. Because I had no place to land, I began to ask God if I should go to Rhode Island and join my family (who did not have a relationship with Christ at the time).

I got no clear answer from God, so I decided to move on to Rhode Island where I had a place to stay. This began a really hard season for me, and to this day I know, looking back, I made the wrong decision. You see, I sought what I perceived was the easy path. I had nowhere to live in Missouri, but I did in Rhode Island. That was it—that was my deciding factor. Forget that when I had lived at home years prior, I was miserable. In Missouri I had a community of godly friends and a great church. In Rhode Island it felt like a spiritual desert. I ended up spending the next six months trying to find a way back to Missouri while living under a spiritual cloud of heaviness. I had lost perspective and purpose.

I share this because I came out of Wyoming with a false sense of security. I had been in a really good place spiritually, and I assumed that coming out of that season would lead to further favor. When I began praying about moving to Rhode Island (which I did not do long), I never heard an answer, so I took the decision into my own hands and chose the easier path. But I failed to take into account all the hardship that could happen. At the end of the day, I never had a green light to go. I took the perceived easy way out only to end up in a tough situation.

If I am being really honest, and I am (sometimes trembling as I do), it was in that season I let my guard down. I began spending a lot of time on the phone with a guy from Wyoming who was not a believer. Feelings began to form. I am thankful that when I finally returned to Missouri and found my groove again, I listened to the conviction I had and cut off the communication.

False security led me to pursue my own will and, thus, led me outside of what I truly believe God had for me next. And it was there, on my own path, that I lost perspective and flirted with temptation. God is gracious and I was able to get back in the race He has called me to run.

Are you getting by on a false sense of security, basing decisions on what you perceive to be best? Perhaps you have prayed only to have no further direction and use that quietness to take matters into your own hands. Ask yourself this: What is your Rhode Island? Where is your false security beckoning you to run?

Creates blinders to the reality around you. When you have an untouchable mindset, you have blinders on that create a tunnel vision of sorts. Or you might identify more with the idea of rose-colored glasses. Either way, reality is distorted.

When I was living in the myth, I had my own blinders and rose-colored glasses. Everything was predictable, set and achievable. But neither of those beliefs was rooted in reality. Each was rooted in false hope and security that left me vulnerable to attacks from the enemy. I was seeing only a portion of life: the portion right in front of me. I could not see how the enemy was working to bring me down on the left and the right. He was working in the shadows, and I was prepared to battle only what was straight ahead.

You could likely have your own blinders that are allowing you to see just a portion of what is really going on. Perhaps they let you view the battle directly in front of you while causing you to miss the battle waging in the spiritual world everywhere else around you. Don't be so preoccupied by the physical circumstances of a broken heart, lost dream or financial strain that you are distracted from the very real and eternal blows the enemy is wanting to make to your soul. Or perhaps you go through life with rose-colored glasses, wanting to believe only the best. While I am an eternal optimist and always hope for the best, there is wisdom in being open to the reality that not everything is good and perfect. That not everything will turn out the way you would like it to or hope it will. Whichever you might be wearing, be wary and open to the possibility that both are hindrances to flourishing in life.

Distracts you from the spiritual disciplines. When you have an untouchable mindset, you lack the fortitude for endurance that comes from exercising the spiritual disciplines. You are not holding firm to some very practical tools that help you combat the untouchable myth.

When I made my own epic fail, I was in a very happy place in life (wearing those rose-colored glasses). But in that season when the relationship was new and captivating, I began to slack on important spiritual disciplines like prayer and Bible reading. I made excuses that I was extra busy that day, or I would rush through my devotions just to say I did them.

There is no exact formula for righteousness, and I am not holding law above grace, but there is value in implementing spiritual disciplines in your life—things like prayer, humility and surrender. First Timothy 4:7–8 encourages us to train in godliness: "Have nothing to do with irreverent, silly myths. Rather train yourself for godliness; for while bodily training is of some value, godliness is of value in every way, as it holds promise for the present life and also for the life to come."

One of my favorite books is *So, You Want to Be Like Christ?* by Charles R. Swindoll (Nelson, 2005). In it he talks about discipline being something that leads to intimacy with Christ:

> Seeking intimacy with the Almighty requires focused determination, demands specific changes in attitude and behavior, and will come with a number of heartbreak and setbacks. . . . So why exercise spiritual disciplines? To know Jesus Christ. They are simply a means by which you come to know Him experientially. By imitating Him, by sharing His experiences, by living life as He lived it, allowing the Holy Spirit to shape you by the disciplines from the inside out, you will become more like Him.

Spiritual disciplines are not meant to be a list of rules but rather a way to train for godliness and become more like Christ. And as you become more like Him, you become less likely to flirt with temptation.

Does not allow you to be open to possibilities. Peter was not open to the possibility of failure, and neither was I. Chances are, neither are you. But when you are not open to the possibility that anything is possible, you stand to lose everything. You stand to fall.

When you buy into the untouchable myth, you are not open to possibilities. You are living in denial, right? Never be so stubborn (and I use a strong word as a reminder to myself!) that you settle for average. That you settle for limited perspective. Be cautiously prepared for every possibility.

Causes you to miss what God has in store for you. If Peter had acknowledged that denying Jesus was possible and prepared accordingly, instead of standing afar with the Roman soldiers, he could have been at Jesus' side in His final hours.

As we have noted, it is safe to bet that Peter wished he would have been by his Savior's side as He suffered for us and conquered death, instead of in the company of those who persecuted and killed Jesus. Peter could have been right there in those pivotal hours, but he was far off in fear. Instead of allowing the untouchable mindset to keep you in the company of opposition, embrace weakness in order to run your race with strength and victory. Be there and show up for your calling. Don't miss an opportunity to be exactly where God wants you.

Lacking Preparation

When you buy into the untouchable myth, many hindrances block your path and keep you from being prepared for what might come. Truth is, you will not be able to dodge the enemy's attacks forever. You will be so preoccupied with jumping hurdles and so weary from the weight of sin trying to cling to you that you will not be freed up to run with endurance.

In the next four chapters we are going to explore the death of the myth. You are going to get valuable tools that will allow you to have freedom from the untouchable mindset and freedom from epic fails in your own life. It is time to get prepared to do battle and live life victoriously!

GOING DEEPER

1. Out of the five hindrances to an untouchable mindset, which one do you struggle with the most? How so?
2. How might you be able to grow in this area? What steps will you begin taking to overcome your hindrance?

CLOSING PRAYER

Father, I am so sorry for when I have allowed things to become a hindrance in pursuing You with all my heart. Will You forgive me? Help me to lay aside the weight and sin that entangles me, so that I might run this race with endurance. Give me victory over any hindrances in my life. I long for You and to hear You say, "Well done, good and faithful servant!" Please help me to run the race well, in the name of Jesus. Amen.

Part 3

THE DEATH
OF THE MYTH

7

The What, Why and How

Jesus answered him, "If anyone loves me, he will keep my
word, and my Father will love him, and we will come to
him and make our home with him."

John 14:23

I t is not enough just to know *what* the untouchable myth is
and how it can affect your life. In order to thrive, you need to
understand *why* it is vital to live your life free from it and *how*
you can combat the mindset. This is the beginning of death for
the untouchable mindset.

The What

You know the what—the theme and the core of this book: It
is that most people, and very likely you, have a list of untouchables. A list of sins so obvious that you believe you will never

commit them. It is a false sense of security to believe you are above certain sins—and you know what those key things are for you. For me one was that I would never have sex outside of marriage. It was an obvious "never go there" sin, and I put it in my cupboard, tucked away and out of sight.

So, what are your untouchables? If you have not yet taken account of them, this would be a good time to do so. In fact, stop now and make your untouchable list. Until you are able to identify the untouchables, you will never be able to stand against them.

Now, let me say something that sounds like just the opposite: Today, I no longer have a list of untouchables. I know the kinds of things that I am most tempted to do, but I also am firmly aware that under the right circumstances, *anything* is possible. Do I want to travel down that path? Of course not! But I am keenly aware that saying I will never do something does not mean I will never do it. This is a place where you want to be as well.

And as we travel along together, you will get there. Then if someone were to ask you to write down a list of things you would never do, you could hand that person a blank piece of paper. Remember, this is not because you plan on doing terrible things, but rather because you realize how vulnerable you really are.

I know this seems contradictory. It seems odd to think you might be capable of, say, robbing a bank—surely that would be a "never" for most Christians, right? But that is just the point. Putting things on the list that you are certain you would never do shows the kinds of things that can most tempt you. You are vulnerable to the types of sins that are written there—or at least some close cousins. You might not rob a bank, but you might rob from your employer to cover the medical bills piling up.

I know you would rather not admit that you could do things like cheat on your taxes or hurt somebody—I would rather not admit that possibility either. But thinking you are exempt from temptation is exactly what leads to doing something you thought you would never do, and that is a dangerous place to be.

The Why

You know the what—you need to be on your guard against any temptation to sin. But have you ever thought about why? Why is it important to guard against sin? Understanding this is immensely valuable to living a life of authenticity and freedom. The how will be an outflow of your why, so it is important you understand this core belief.

First and foremost, you guard against sin because you *love God*. Second, you guard against sin in order to *set an example*. And third, you take a stand against sin because you want to *protect your testimony*.

Love God. Your driving force for everything in life should be your love for God. Deep and personal love for your Savior. Without that kind of love, why would you want to live a life dedicated to His purposes?

I want to pause here because this point is incredibly important. Without a relationship with Christ, none of this really matters. So before we move forward, I want to extend an opportunity for you to have that relationship if you do not have it now.

If you have not made Jesus Lord of your life and embraced His gift of salvation, read 2 Corinthians 6:2. This tells you that now is the appointed hour and now is the day of salvation for you! He loves you so much that He died very painfully for you by a punishment He did not deserve. He longs for relationship with you. It is not enough to be a good person; you must be willing to give your life completely over to God. How do you do that? Confess your sins and invite Jesus into your life as Lord and Savior, committing it all to Him!

This is a foundation you must lay before anything else can be built. This is where a flourishing life is birthed. So if you desire to live a life in freedom and apart from sin, do it first and foremost because you love God. Jesus said in John 14:23 that if you love God, you will keep His commands. If you truly love God, His desires will become yours, and a longing to do what is right in His eyes will take precedence over your desires of the flesh.

Set an example. When you love God and live for Him, your life becomes an example for others. You begin to reflect Him in your attitude, words and decisions in a way that makes it obvious He is first in your life.

Those who live for God often are recognized as having something "different" about them. People wonder why they are so full of joy in difficult times and encouraging to others in their own storms. You become an example to others around you. And perhaps maybe, just maybe, they will want what you have.

Paul told people to follow him as he followed Christ (see 1 Corinthians 11:1). Why is it important to refrain from sin or even the hint of it? Because as a follower of Christ you become an example. Be the person who sets such a great example that you can confidently invite others to follow you.

When I spent that summer in Wyoming, my greatest fear was that I would not be able to form relationships with the co-workers I spent time with each day. Would I act self-righteous? Or be too passive about my faith?

Every evening that summer I was surrounded by people who held philosophies different from my own. The three friends I spent most of my time with were living for the things of this world. Then there was a handful of Muslims I talked to regularly about religion. The guy who cooked our meals was a vocal atheist, and the wranglers I sat next to at lunch were devoted Mormons. The realities for me that summer might not describe your immediate surroundings, but they do describe the world we live in.

So how did this melting pot of worldviews play out for me? I chose to love and serve those around me; I chose to be an example.

Little things like wiping up someone's spilt beer or making a birthday card for a co-worker or clearing dinner plates from the table made an impact. I could hardly believe people even noticed! When people see someone willing to serve others, they pay attention because the world is not accustomed to this.

More often than not it is your example that piques the interest of an unbeliever. Choose righteousness so that others may be encouraged to live the same way.

Protect your testimony. Living a righteous life allows you to protect your testimony. Truth be told, I wish I could take back my epic mistakes in order to protect my testimony, to be the kind of person people cannot point to as a reason why Christians are hypocrites. I have had unbelievers throw even the smallest mistakes in my face. How could I not want to protect my testimony with that in mind? Don't give unbelievers a reason to discount the power of God because of your actions as a Christian.

Refrain from sin so that you can protect your calling and your testimony. Then use that testimony as a vehicle for God's purposes and draw others to Him.

The How

In the next three chapters I will give you three ways you can combat the untouchable myth: You must admit weakness, put on the armor of God and establish guardrails.

But first I would like to address one way you can create a barrier between you and the untouchable myth: *accountability*. You can dive into the experience we are about to explore, but you cannot do it on your own. God created us for relationship and community; this support system exists for us for both the good and the bad.

Jessica, when sharing her story, points to the importance of accountability in her life. Jessica grew up going to church faithfully in Minnesota and was the girl who did all the right things. She spent her adolescent years in the Fine Arts ministry, a national program to help youth develop their gifts and passions, and served on the worship team at her church.

All the while Jessica was striving to serve God in her youth, she was also struggling secretly with porn and masturbation. This is the stronghold I knew all too well, and one that, quite frankly, more women struggle with than you might think.

After fighting against the stronghold alone and unsuccessfully for many years, Jessica finally reached out to a few close friends for accountability. She found enormous benefit and blessing in her journey to have people she could lean on and share her struggles with. People she could trust. It was exactly what she needed to persevere and break free.

Jessica's struggle did not end there, however. After meeting an attractive guy, she entered into a dating relationship. She thought he was spiritually strong and good. Unfortunately, Jessica soon discovered he was not the man she thought he was, because, although he seemed like a good Christian on the outside, behind closed doors she felt that he was manipulative and controlling. She felt pressured to do things she was not prepared for or comfortable with, and Jessica soon began to compromise. It was not long before they had sex for the first time.

Jessica was in that unhealthy relationship for a while before the two finally separated. In the meantime, she had grown disconnected from her church, lacked community and, more than anything, felt distant from God.

After the breakup Jessica's parents spoke with her to share their concern. They cared about her quality of life and where her heart was. After talking with them she realized that she craved the trust and accountability of a Christian community.

After a few months of counseling and easing back into ministry, Jessica is now flourishing as a worship leader in her church. Her sweet nature and passion for Jesus are beautifully evident in her life today!

Those gaps of sin and aloneness over the years were hard for Jessica, even dark at times. But today her life looks a lot brighter. She loves to speak of God's grace and redemption. It was obvious, as I listened to her tell her story, that having godly people around her whom she could trust was important to her healing. Community and accountability were part of her overcoming and working through her dark days.

No man is an island. We cannot successfully navigate the challenges we face as believers without a strong, godly community around us, including a few close friends. Find a couple of people who love God and whom you can trust to share your journey with you. People who can safely bring you back into the light when they see you drifting. Friends who will both love you and hold you accountable through the highs and lows, helping you grow more into the likeness of Christ. And you can do the same for them.

Now that we have that established, are you up for the challenge? Are you ready to explore your weaknesses, put on the armor you need for battle and set up boundaries? Time to grasp the practical tools you need for a flourishing life that stands apart from the untouchable myth!

—————————————| GOING DEEPER |—————————————

1. Did you make your list of untouchables? If not, take time to account for those now. What are your thoughts on this list after having read what you have read so far? Is it still crazy to fathom you would do even one of those items on the list? Or can you see how admitting the possibility might actually help you guard against doing so?

2. Do you have accountability in your life? Who is that godly person you can be honest with? If you do not have someone, what person in your life might be willing to help you with accountability?

—————————————| CLOSING PRAYER |—————————————

O God, may my why be genuine and wholehearted. Everything I do, I do because I love You. Because You are everything. I pray my why would never become polluted or misdirected. Help me to live with focused purpose that is an overflow of a healthy why. God, You are my intimate Friend, sustainer through temptation and protector from sin. Thank You for Your consistency; that I can always count on You. You are worthy of all praise! Amen.

8

Flourishing by Admitting Weakness

He gives strength to the weary and increases the power
of the weak.

Isaiah 40:29 NIV

Weakness plagues us all, heroes and villains alike.
Achilles and his heel. Superman and kryptonite.
Gollum and the golden ring. Green Lantern and
the color yellow (yes, that's legit). Lord Voldemort and his Hor-
cruxes. In the fictional world, no amount of power can free one
from a weakness.

If weakness is evident in a world of make-believe where anything is possible, we humans are not going to escape an Achilles'
heel either. Every man, woman and child has a weakness, because
none of us is immortal or perfect. It is supposed that the mighty
Genghis Khan, ruler of the Mongol Empire, died from injuries

sustained after being thrown from a horse. Alexander the Great died at the age of 32, probably from a fever.

Weakness is a natural part of humanity. But this does not mean it has to be a bad thing. In fact, if addressed and brought to the surface to be dealt with, weakness can be a great conduit for growth. It is when weakness is kept in the shadows and buried in the recesses of the soul that it becomes dangerous.

While the untouchable myth is a hindrance, oddly enough, weakness is a good thing when it can be admitted. Unfortunately, the opposite seems to be true in our society. Too many people go through life with a tough exterior without any intention of revealing weakness; they believe weakness is a bad thing. That it must be kept suppressed. That it cannot be talked about. Weakness is a vulnerability that cannot be afforded.

I have struggled with a fear of weakness for much of my life. I believed for a long time that weakness was to be avoided, and I lived with a tough exterior to counteract any perception of vulnerability. I did not like asking people for help or sharing my feelings. As a result I kept people at a distance because I wanted them to see strength in me. I wanted to be strong and dependable. I have come a long way, but to this day I still find moments when admitting weakness or the need for help is hard. Even when I was pregnant, I had a difficult time asking for help to lift boxes or admitting I did not feel good and needed a break. It is hard to admit weakness for many of us, if we are honest.

Yet the truth is—and many never realize—that weakness opens the door to preparation. When weakness can be addressed, we are allowed the freedom to manage it properly. *We flourish in life when we admit weakness.*

As we saw earlier, Jason experienced this truth in his addiction to pornography. He was afraid to admit weakness—to share his struggle with someone and ask for help. Instead he tried to work through his problem alone. Coming out on the other side of his epic fail, he testifies that being able to admit weakness is vital to living a flourishing life.

Are you in a place where you can admit weakness? Are you willing to be open to the possibility that by doing so you are actually being strong? There must be a shift in your mindset that admitting weakness is a strength. I know from experience that this is not easy but necessary. But by admitting your weakness(es), you give yourself room to prepare for what may come. You are better able to see potential pitfalls ahead of you and make plans to avoid them. Without the ability to admit weakness—to see those potential pitfalls—you are unable to guard against them.

Strength in Weakness

On Twitter Simon Sinek wrote, "True strength is the courage to admit our weaknesses." There was a time in my life that I was afraid to confront my weaknesses because I thought if I did, I lacked strength. Yet true strength has no such fear. True strength is assurance and confidence: You know who you are; you understand what you are capable of doing and not doing; and you recognize that to travel through life successfully you must not do it alone.

After Paul struggled in prayer with his "thorn in the flesh," he came to this life-changing conclusion:

> But [Jesus] said to me, "My grace is sufficient for you, for my power is made perfect in weakness." Therefore I will boast all the more gladly of my weaknesses, so that the power of Christ

may rest upon me. For the sake of Christ, then, I am content with weaknesses, insults, hardships, persecutions, and calamities. For when I am weak, then I am strong.

2 Corinthians 12:9–10

Weakness can be a good thing—we have established that, right? It is something we must leave room for if we are to flourish. The wonderful news is that weakness does not have to lead to an epic fail—because that is what we believe about weakness: that it opens our lives to failure. But the truth is, the more you can own your weakness, the greater God's strength can show up in your life. Ignoring weakness is not strength; rather, being able to admit weakness is where strength truly lies.

Paul nailed this in 2 Corinthians. He even went to the extent of boasting in his weaknesses because he preferred the power of Christ. Paul understood that weakness made room for God to show up, to work and to be made famous.

Matthew Henry, in his *Commentary on the Whole Bible* (Hendrickson, 1994), discusses this passage:

This is a Christian paradox: when we are weak in ourselves, then we are strong in the grace of our Lord Jesus Christ; when we see ourselves weak in ourselves, then we go out of ourselves to Christ, and are qualified to receive strength from him, and experience most of the supplies of divine strength and grace.

It is a shift in our modern mindset. Admitting weakness is hard for all of us, but when we do this, we actually activate strength through the power of God. Truth is, you cannot go through this life in your own strength. You will fall and, potentially, fall hard. It is time to stop living out of what you think you are capable of doing and start operating out of a mindset that you need to lean on a greater source of strength. Let go of the reins and take hold of the supernatural strength and grace God supplies.

Honestly, it is such a relief when you can reach this point. You no longer feel the pressure to keep it all together. You no longer tear yourself up over depletion or exhaustion. The expectation to maintain perfection crumbles at the feet of humility. When you can embrace weakness and allow God's strength to take over—to fill in the gaps—there is freedom to flourish. How could you not want that!

Can you boast in your weakness? Are you able to admit that you need the power of God? Realizing this will be a turning point for you because it activates in your life what only God can do. *You are limited, but He is limitless.* Which will you choose?

Anything Is Possible

Anything is possible. We often look at that phrase with hope and optimism. *Anything is possible*—I could meet my spouse today or unexpectedly get a promotion or perhaps win the lottery. Anything is possible!

Have you looked at this phrase from a different perspective? Anything is possible—a fall or stumble is possible. A sin you never thought you would commit is possible. Remember: You are not above anything.

I am not sharing these thoughts in order to instill fear in your heart but to open your eyes: *Anything is possible.* Do you think that young, hopeful, godly David approached the throne with the idea that he would later commit adultery and murder? That wise King Solomon imagined he would fall so far as to indulge in hundreds of wives and concubines? That faithful prophet Jonah expected to run in the direction opposite of God's call on his life? That Peter would deny his Savior? That the high-profile pastors who have fallen in recent years predicted they would succumb to alcoholism, affairs, addiction and more?

Do you think any one of the above believed these acts were possible? Probably not. They most likely envisioned following God faithfully without wavering or compromising their beliefs, staying strong and above reproach. But somewhere along the line they ignored the possibility of failure and lived life out of their own strength. It was when they became secure in their own abilities and coasted on complacency that temptation led to sin. Their failure to admit weakness led to their weaknesses being targeted, and, ultimately, this led to a downward spiral.

So, do you believe that you are untouchable? Or do you believe that anything is possible? These two very different trains of thought will direct your life toward two very different paths. Choosing to believe that you are not above anything gives you strength—the power of knowledge—to know that you are vulnerable. When you know you are vulnerable, you can guard yourself. You can prepare, and that is strength.

Embrace that anything is possible—the good and the bad—not out of pessimism but out of a realistic perspective that you are weak and that you need God's strength to face whatever temptation may come your way.

Weakness Prepares

You might be asking yourself, "So, how *does* admitting weakness allow me to flourish in life?" When you admit weakness, you can prepare for whatever may come your way. When you have this mindset, you can take hold of the tools needed to face temptation. You can see your need for help and plan ahead. Most importantly, when you know you are weak, you can make room for God's strength to show up! This is vital for overcoming an untouchable mindset.

Remember: Vulnerability is strength. Admitting where you fall short or have limitations leads to freedom. Accepting these truths will take the weight off your shoulders to have it all together. With this new outlook you crave the strength that God provides in your weakness. You no longer feel the need to put on a show or have it all together; the stress is lifted from you, and you can flourish in your weakness because God is at work in this place.

The first step, then, in guarding against the untouchable myth is to admit weakness. To be open to the possibility that you are not untouchable. To realize you are a human wrapped in flesh, prone to sin, in need of a Savior to strengthen you for righteousness.

In the next two chapters, we will explore the next two steps you must take in order to walk in victory over the myth that you are too faithful to fall. By the end of this book, I pray you will be able to combat temptation and flourish in life!

─────────────┤ GOING DEEPER ├─────────────

1. Do you struggle with being vulnerable or admitting weakness? If so, where might this tension stem from? For me it was the unbalance I saw between my quiet mother and authoritative father. Where did such an outlook start

for you, and can you identify how this might actually be unhealthy?

2. Do you think you can truly come to a place of admitting weakness? And do you believe that you can actually flourish in this place?

———————————| CLOSING PRAYER |———————————

Father, I am so sorry for the times I have tried to do things out of my own strength. It's exhausting trying to keep it all together and I'm done. I no longer want to try to accomplish anything on my own. Help me to see the end of my strength each time I forget this prayer and start tapping into myself. Help me to seek instead Your supernatural strength. To go to You. I admit my weaknesses so that Your strength may shine. So that You might be glorified in my life! May Your strength be made perfect in my weakness. Amen.

9

The Armor of God

Finally, be strong in the Lord and in the strength of his might. Put on the whole armor of God, that you may be able to stand against the schemes of the devil. For we do not wrestle against flesh and blood, but against the rulers, against the authorities, against the cosmic powers over this present darkness, against the spiritual forces of evil in the heavenly places. Therefore take up the whole armor of God, that you may be able to withstand in the evil day, and having done all, to stand firm. Stand therefore, having fastened on the belt of truth, and having put on the breastplate of righteousness, and, as shoes for your feet, having put on the readiness given by the gospel of peace. In all circumstances take up the shield of faith, with which you can extinguish all the flaming darts of the evil one; and take the helmet of salvation, and the sword of the Spirit, which is the word of God, praying at all times in the Spirit, with all prayer and supplication. To that end, keep alert with all perseverance, making supplication for

all the saints, and also for me, that words may be given to
me in opening my mouth boldly to proclaim the mystery
of the gospel, for which I am an ambassador in chains,
that I may declare it boldly, as I ought to speak.

Ephesians 6:10–20

In 2011 Sgt. Timothy Gilboe was serving in an infantry regiment of the United States Army in the Wardak Province in Afghanistan. While conducting a patrol in the streets of a local village, his platoon came under direct fire.

When he and the squad leader, Staff Sgt. Matthew Hermanson, spotted two insurgents around the corner of a building, Hermanson directed Gilboe to stay behind him as they ran forward.

Hermanson was mortally wounded in the gunfire that followed. When Gilboe had to put down his machine gun in order to deal with flames near a rucksack filled with ammunition, the two insurgents charged again. A fellow soldier was able to get a line of fire on one of the insurgents, and Gilboe, unable to grab his weapon, charged the other, grabbing the barrel of the enemy's AK-47 and forcing the muzzle to his own chest plate.

The insurgent fired upon Gilboe at point-blank range. Though the blast knocked Gilboe to the ground and pelted his legs with shrapnel, he was able to get to his feet, throw aside the enemy's weapon and wrestle in hand-to-hand combat until a fellow soldier could shoot and kill the insurgent.

Gilboe was able to clear the area and provide first aid to wounded soldiers until medics arrived. His actions are credited with saving the lives of at least two soldiers.

Sergeant Gilboe credits his life to Sergeant Hermanson and to his armor. Without either, Gilboe says he likely would not be here today.

Armor helps protect soldiers from enemy fire and saves lives. Just as physical armor saves lives, so does spiritual armor. Over and over again, God gives us insight into the spiritual battle we face. Our fight is not against flesh and blood but against spiritual forces we cannot see. In his *Bible Exposition Commentary* (Victor Books, 1996), Warren W. Wiersbe writes, "Throughout the entire Bible, God instructs us about the enemy, so there is no reason for us to be caught off guard." In light of this truth, you and I must be ready to go to battle not with physical weapons but with spiritual weapons.

In the spiritual battle that is taking place all around you, you will not win in your own strength and by your own means. If you are going to win against the untouchable myth, you must be willing to fight with spiritual weapons—the armor of God.

In this chapter you are going to learn how to put on the whole armor of God. With these weapons you fight the spiritual battle not on your own but in God's strength. One thing I hope you have learned so far is that you need God in order to flourish in life. You cannot fight the spiritual battle and have victory over the enemy without His help.

First and foremost, the armor of God is a tool put on by active faith. If you are going to take on this protection, you need living faith—faith that is activated each and every day. You cannot overcome the enemy and stand firm against temptation with passive faith. If you are committed to this battle, you must also commit to living each day out of a place of active faith.

What does this mean exactly? Well, it means having faith each day in God, knowing who He is and what He has done.

God is the beginning and the end; He is all-powerful. You can have confidence that He is the ultimate authority and with great celebration declare that Jesus conquered death. Because He has won the victory, you have victory! Remember, "If God is for us, who can be against us?" (Romans 8:31). You are not alone in your battle; God is for you and with you. He brings victory over the enemy—already won on the cross!—into your situation.

The Armor of God

The armor of God as described in Ephesians 6 is structured like the armor used in ancient times. Paul uses this analogy to describe the kind of offense and defense you need on a daily basis in order to stand firm against the enemy's schemes. Let's take a look at each piece and how to use it.

First, he describes the *belt of truth*. Something important to know about the belt of the armor: It holds the rest of the gear together. Without the belt, the armor falls apart. This means that truth is vital to your protection and to being victorious. If Satan is a liar, and indeed he is, you must embrace truth. If you will be led by truth, then you will be able to defeat the enemy when an attack comes your way.

Temptation is all around you and deception along with it. In order to stand against deception, find God's truth. It will not fail you when the liar attempts to deceive you.

Another interesting thing about the belt is that the scabbard, the sheath that holds the sword—in this case the sword of the Spirit—hangs from it. Which means, without the belt of truth you cannot carry your only offensive tool—the sword of the Spirit, which is the Word of God. Embrace truth and carry the Word of God with you.

The *breastplate of righteousness* is a protective covering. When you are living a righteous life in Christ, you are living a life that does not compromise on integrity.

Satan is called the accuser in the Bible, and we are told he brings charges against God's people. In the book of Job, we read that Satan went before God to find fault with the man. In Zechariah 3:1, Satan stands before God to accuse high priest Joshua. Satan is looking for an opportunity to trip you up so that he can go before God and accuse you. He wants to be able to go to God, point at you and say you are not worthy of God's love. Never give him room to do so!

A righteous life is a protective measure against accusation. Without righteousness, Satan has an easier job of calling you out. But with it, you are covered and guarded against his threats.

With the *shoes of the Gospel*, you wear peace—peace that is received from the Gospel. When you put on these shoes each day, you are putting on peace. And not just peace with yourself but also peace with others—because when you walk in the Gospel, which is peace, you are bringing the Gospel to others.

Isaiah 52:7 declares, "How beautiful upon the mountains are the feet of him who brings good news, who publishes peace, who brings good news of happiness, who publishes salvation, who says to Zion, 'Your God reigns.'"

You must carry with you the peace of the Gospel and share it with others so that you may withstand whatever the enemy brings against you.

A tool you must carry with you each day is the *shield of faith*. Faith, as we noted at the beginning of this chapter, is a necessary piece of the armor of God. Daily you must make a decision to operate out of active faith, faith that breathes and lives. Without faith you are vulnerable to spiritual attacks. Without the shield of faith, the fiery darts from the enemy will eventually hit you.

In ancient times a shield was a protective measure against the enemy's weapons for every soldier. Interestingly enough, it was also designed to fit alongside other shields so that, as a collective group, all the soldiers had greater defense. Know that you do not have to fight alone. Take up the shield of faith and surround yourself with other believers so that together you are stronger:

> Two are better than one, because they have a good reward for their toil. For if they fall, one will lift up his fellow. But woe to him who is alone when he falls and has not another to lift him up! Again, if two lie together, they keep warm, but how can one keep warm alone? And though a man might prevail against one who is alone, two will withstand him—a threefold cord is not quickly broken.
>
> Ecclesiastes 4:9–12

You are stronger with a community around you. Remember Jessica's story and how accountability was important as she worked through her struggles? Lock shields with others in the Body of Christ, and you will be able to stand against the enemy's offense.

You must also wear the *helmet of salvation*. This is very important because much of the battle is waged in your mind. This is why it is vital to have the mind of Christ. If you are led by Him in your mind, Satan cannot lure you away.

One of the verses I recite to myself most often comes from the book of Colossians: "Since, then, you have been raised with Christ, set your hearts on things above, where Christ is, seated at the right hand of God. Set your minds on things above, not on earthly things" (Colossians 3:1–2 NIV).

Like a lot of people I tend to live in my mind. I am there constantly and sometimes forget to share what is going on in there with others. (Just ask my husband. Sorry, babe!) Oftentimes there is a whole battle going on in your head that is a real struggle, even if everything on the outside seems cool and collected. A hidden battle of deception, negativity and impure thoughts. This is why it is important to "take every thought captive to obey Christ" (2 Corinthians 10:5) and keep your mind focused on what is above—so that the enemy cannot get ahold of it.

Few books have had such a profound impact on my life as *Battlefield of the Mind* (Warner, 1995) has. In it Joyce Meyer shares this:

> If something is ministering death to you, don't do it any longer. When certain lines of thought fill you full of death, you know immediately that it is not the mind of the Spirit. . . . It is very helpful to the believer to learn to discern life and death within himself. Jesus has made arrangements for us to be filled with life by putting his own mind in us. We can choose to flow in the mind of Christ.

You have been given a new mind, renewed in the Spirit. You have been given His mind! Choose life-giving thoughts and rebuke those that bring death.

This is why Colossians 3:1–2 is so vital to my spiritual walk and, I venture to say, should be to yours as well. Anytime you have an attack in your mind—anytime the enemy begins to whisper his lies in there—recite this verse. Remind yourself that your thoughts should be on what is above. On the lovely and beautiful. On the victorious reign of Christ.

All of this starts with salvation. If you have not given your life to Jesus, you will not be able to have victory in your mind. Start there and then you can pursue a mind fixed on God. This is also why you must spend time studying the Bible. In there you will find your tool of defense. Start with salvation, and then you can "grow in the grace and knowledge of our Lord and Savior Jesus Christ. To him be the glory both now and to the day of eternity. Amen" (2 Peter 3:18).

The last thing you must carry with you is the *sword of the Spirit*. It is the only offensive piece in all the armor, which makes it incredibly important. To carry the sword with you means to be consumed by the Word of God. Without it, you lack a crucial weapon in your fight against the tempter.

Before Jesus began His earthly ministry, He spent forty days in the desert. It was there Satan attacked Jesus and tried to cause Him to stumble. Satan even used Scripture to try to trip Jesus! But Jesus knew the Bible, setting an example of how important it is to know the Word of God. Three times Satan tried to tempt Jesus to sin, and three times Jesus fought back with Scripture.

Without the armor of God, you are incredibly vulnerable to attacks. This is why you must choose to put it on each day.

In Addition

Paul does not stop with the armor. He continues by encouraging us to pray "at all times." We have a similar direction in 1 Thessalonians 5:17, which says that we must "pray without ceasing." Some look at that and feel immediately discouraged, because how is one supposed to pray without ceasing? I breathed a sigh of relief when I learned it does not mean to pray without stopping; rather, it is describing a lifestyle of prayer. Your days should be filled with instances of prayer—in your devotional time in the morning, in your car, in the midst of a problem popping up or when you are sitting down for a meal. Prayer should be the natural outflow of a life committed to following Christ.

Prayer brings us closer to God and nurtures intimacy with Him. It also energizes the soldier—it energizes you! Moses prayed while his people fought a battle (see Exodus 17:8–16). In fact, he prayed until the battle was won. Prayer must be part of your daily walk. You certainly do not want to be unprepared when your next battle comes.

Remember how we learned that Peter lacked prayer in those final hours before Jesus' death? Let that be a clear picture of what failure to pray can leave room for when temptation comes—defeat. You and I must be prayer warriors if we want to see victory in our battles.

Paul also encourages us to keep alert with perseverance. This is key to winning a battle. Anyone who begins to tire and gives up will lose the battle against spiritual forces. So don't give up or lose heart. Trust God and embrace endurance.

Jesus as Our Armor

The armor of God is something you decide to put on each day. By faith you take each piece and put it on. But the armor is also a picture of who Jesus is. Jesus is . . .

> *Truth*—"Jesus said to him, 'I am the way, and the truth, and the life. No one comes to the Father except through me'" (John 14:6).

Righteousness—"In those days and at that time I will cause a righteous Branch of David to spring forth; and He shall execute justice and righteousness on the earth" (Jeremiah 33:15 NASB).

Peace—"For he himself is our peace, who has made us both one and has broken down in his flesh the dividing wall of hostility" (Ephesians 2:14).

Faithfulness—"Let us hold fast the confession of our hope without wavering, for he who promised is faithful" (Hebrews 10:23).

Savior—"And there is salvation in no one else, for there is no other name under heaven that has been given among men by which we must be saved" (Acts 4:12).

The Word of God—"It is they [the Scriptures] that bear witness about me" (John 5:39).

The armor we are called to put on each day requires faith in Jesus Christ—faith that Jesus is who He says He is. He is central to everything! Our faith . . . our lives . . . our actions . . . our choices. Jesus is central to everything in our lives. Without Him there, everything else is off. Without Him there, fighting Satan is an impossible task.

The words found in Matthew 6:33 echo this call beautifully: "Seek first the kingdom of God and his righteousness, and all these things will be added to you." Seek God and the things close to His heart first, and those things will be close to your heart as well. Not only that, but everything else in your life will be taken care of. Is Jesus the center of your life? Do you consider Him your priority?

Being able to admit weakness is the first step in combatting the untouchable mindset; adding the armor of God to your daily wardrobe is the necessary second step. If the idea of mastering each piece in one day is daunting, try growing in each area one at a time. Choose to have active faith that puts on each piece of the armor every day and be prepared for any spiritual battle that might come your way, whether that battle is obvious or not . . . and especially if not. It is the untouchables that sneak up on you without warning. Unprepared and unguarded, you will fall to them. But if you are wearing the armor of God, you are in a good place to overcome and have victory!

GOING DEEPER

1. Which piece of armor would you benefit from most in implementing? Which do you struggle with most and could you be more intentional about putting on each day?

2. What steps will you take to clothe yourself in this piece of armor every day? If you choose the shoes of the Gospel, for example, how might you take steps toward peace with others in your expression of the Good News?

CLOSING PRAYER

God, I thank You that You are my sustainer and everything I could possibly need is found in You. I know there is a very real spiritual battle going on for my soul, and I'm so grateful You do not leave me alone and unprepared to fight it. Show me how I can better prepare each day and be intentional about stepping into the armor of God. With Your strength and victory, I know I can be strong, too. I pray that not only will I flourish over the enemy but also that You, Christ, would be glorified in my life. Let others see You, Jesus. Amen.

10

Establishing Guardrails

Above all else, guard your heart, for everything you do
flows from it.

Proverbs 4:23 NIV

One thing I learned from my years of failure was the importance of establishing guardrails. These are boundaries you set in place to protect you from straying off the path and getting hurt. How else do we guard our hearts, unless we are able to identify ways to protect ourselves? If your desire is to stay healthy and vibrant, part of doing that is finding ways to keep the unlovely out. Establish boundaries to protect your heart, for out of a healthy heart, life flows.

Side note: I am not talking about closing your heart off. Indeed, your heart should remain open to receive love, forgiveness and hope. An open heart belongs to those with a flourishing life. To guard your heart means to protect it from that which would harm it; to protect it from getting hurt and being defiled.

If you fail to guard your heart, you leave the door open. So, as a precaution, learning to establish guardrails will allow you to protect something incredibly valuable.

I did have my list of don'ts to follow, but I never really learned what it meant to establish healthy, practical boundaries to protect me from going to those don'ts. It was not anyone else's fault, either; in fact, I never even thought to have boundaries in areas I perceived to be untouchable, so I have no one to blame but myself. Certainly I knew some basic don'ts, such as not being alone in the house together, but I lacked deeper understanding to the importance of boundaries and a resolve not to get too close.

Guardrails are important because they keep you in the lane you are meant to follow. When you are driving late at night and taking those curves in the dark, guardrails serve as a safety feature. Without them there to mark the way and keep you on the road, you are in danger.

You need them in life, too. Establishing guardrails keeps you on a safe path away from evil, which leads to death. Putting them in place keeps you from wandering off track.

The Importance of Guardrails

I had a friend years ago who was beginning to put his life back together after a painful divorce. He had recently left his home and everything behind to start over.

This man never imagined he would one day be divorced. He and his wife were Christians and very involved in their local church. She often made trips with fellow volunteers, riding with a married man. One day my friend learned that his wife and the man she carpooled with were having an affair.

A long time ago I knew someone who was given access to a work debit card. Months later it was discovered she had made thousands of dollars of personal purchases with it. This fun-loving person, outwardly on fire for God, shocked many with her hidden spending habit using money from work.

Then there is me, the 25-year-old ministry leader who slept with her boyfriend. Or Jason, the pastor with a porn addiction. Jessica, the young worshiper with multiple strongholds.

Sadly, these are just a few of the many stories I know of Christians who found themselves in sin or on the receiving end of a poor choice they never imagined possible. These people had no idea they would end up doing what they did. One very important factor led to each destructive choice: They lacked guardrails. They were not protected. Had they been, their stories could have looked very different. Marriages would not have been destroyed and jobs would not have been lost. Most importantly, people would not have been hurt.

Establishing guardrails is key to remaining strong against temptation. Without them you are trying to walk in the dark while expecting not to trip, which is rarely possible. If you want to flourish in the calling God has placed on your life, you will have to do this. It will not be easy, but it could save your life from a massive epic fail that would hurt not only you, but also those around you.

Let's explore how to set up this important safeguard.

Establishing Guardrails

So, how do you set up guardrails? What does it look like to implement them? Here are a few tips to help you navigate the process.

Identify Your Areas of Weakness

Search me, O God, and know my heart! Try me and know my thoughts! And see if there be any grievous way in me, and lead me in the way everlasting!

Psalm 139:23–24

First, you must be willing to admit weakness and to identify areas that might hold potential pitfalls. You might not think you will ever have an affair, but are you spending time alone with a married co-worker outside of work? That is a potential pitfall. You probably assume you will never steal from your job, but if you are being left alone with company money, that is a potential pitfall. The right circumstances will pressure anyone to do anything.

Honest reflection is important, and without it you might miss where your weakness lies. Set aside some time with God and ask Him to examine your heart and bring to the surface anything that might be a struggle for you. It can be hard and scary, but the vulnerability will expose what is harmful and protect you and those you love from a world of hurt. Once you can identify where you struggle the most, you will be able to establish how to avoid going there.

Make a List

"Again, when a wicked man turns away from his wickedness which he has committed and practices justice and righteousness, he will save his life. Because he considered and turned away from all his transgressions which he had committed, he shall surely live; he shall not die."

Ezekiel 18:27–28 NASB

Now that you know where your weaknesses are, it is time to brainstorm some ways you can avoid pitfalls. Make a list of your weaknesses or potential problem areas. Then, under each item, make a list of things you can do to protect yourself. No matter how much you dislike the guardrail or how inconvenient it might be, put it down.

If, for example, you struggle with physical boundaries, you probably need to make sure you are never in a room alone with someone you are tempted to go too far with. If you struggle with commitment, you probably need not to date for a while and work through why that might be. Or if anger is your stronghold, go through some counseling and develop a process for stopping anger in its tracks.

Guardrails are not meant to be convenient; they are meant to be protective. Avoiding sin must have a do-whatever-it-takes attitude! Although being tempted is not the same as sinning, the principle in Ezekiel still stands. Examine your weaknesses and turn toward righteousness.

Guard Your Life

Therefore, to one who knows the right thing to do and does not do it, to him it is sin.

James 4:17 NASB

Once you have identified your weaknesses and made a list of how to avoid them, it is time to start putting up protective barriers. It is one thing to know what to do and a completely other thing actually to do it. If you know what you need to do to guard your life and never do it, you are playing with danger.

Let's be honest: Temptation can be exciting. Its lure is strong, but it is also deceptive. Temptation may be fun and perhaps seem innocent, but play with it for very long and you will soon regret it. Temptation can lead to sin, and sin destroys. It hurts. It brings regret and shame. Don't trade peace with yourself and others for momentary sensation.

If you want to flourish in life, protect yourself. There is freedom in obedience!

Stick with It

Watch over your heart with all diligence, for from it flow the springs of life.

Proverbs 4:23 NASB

It is a fact that the enemy does not want you to flourish; he does not want you to set guardrails in place. He will do whatever it takes to wear you down, discourage you and get you to give up.

Are you going to let him? Or are you going to live the flourishing life God desires for you? You can either struggle in sin or pursue a life well lived for the glory of God. Set up your guardrails and prepare to watch over yourself with due diligence. Stay true to the path of righteousness, and life will flow abundantly through you.

Don't Get Too Close

A question I have heard often over the years is, "How close can I get before it's a sin?"

Buzzzzz.

Wrong approach! This is not about how close can you get before it is a sin; this is about how far can you stay away so that you are beyond reproach.

A guardrail is not meant to be placed right up against the sin zone. A guardrail on a highway through the mountains is not perched at the edge of the cliff; it is placed on the area of buffer between the road and the cliff. Still, you should not get too close to that buffer zone. A fall might be possible.

How do you know if you are setting your guardrail too close to a fall? Here are a few key indicators:

1. *You are acting different.* If you find yourself acting a bit unusual or different from your normal, it could be a sign you are heading in a dangerous direction. Maybe you start going to church less often or experiment with activities that are out of the norm. If your usual behavior begins to shift toward a less honorable direction, take notice of this behavior immediately and get back on the road.

2. *You begin to compromise.* For me, I look back and see compromises I made. Ryan and I had a rule that we would not be alone in the house together; however, we allowed a false sense of security to compromise our boundary. When his roommates were home we would go into his room and shut the door. Falsely we believed we were okay because technically we were not in the house alone, yet that did little to help guard against temptation when we were behind a closed door. When you begin making compromises—even little ones—because it is "more convenient" or "not a big deal," you are on the verge of crashing through your guardrail into a bad experience.

3. *You are being pressured by others.* Peer pressure is a great indicator that you are hanging out with the wrong people and that your group needs to change. Peer pressure often leads to a bad choice you will regret. If you are feeling pressure from those around you to do something you would not normally do, take note that it is time for a change in community. Or job. Or relationship.

4. *You tell a lie or feel the need to hide something.* Lying is a sure indicator that you are driving closer and closer to the edge. You are moving close to compromise. Once you start lying or hiding, it usually turns into a series of lies in order to keep up with the original one. Before you know it, you are diving into a deep pit of deception.

5. *You are wondering if an action is right.* Are you questioning whether or not it would be okay to go on that road trip with your boyfriend? Do you think it might be wrong to keep the secret for a co-worker who is stealing? If there is any question or doubt in your mind regarding what you are doing or are about to do, it is probably not a good idea. Consider the warning light going off on your dashboard. You are perilously close to the edge.

Extra Boost

Looking for an added boost to set up guardrails for your journey? Find some accountability! After my own moral failure, I surrounded myself with friends who would ask me the hard questions and call me out if I began to get too close.

Find one or two people who are godly and whom you trust to keep you accountable in potential areas of weakness. People you can be honest with who will help you walk through the journey righteously.

Take Proverbs 13:20 to heart: "Whoever walks with the wise becomes wise, but the companion of fools will suffer harm." Never underestimate the power of a good, godly friend to be a powerful influence for wisdom and good in your life.

Although implementing guardrails may seem difficult or inconvenient, there are few things that will actually benefit you more. Some could argue that they are limitations, but the truth is just the opposite. Proper boundaries give you the freedom to live victoriously and vibrantly!

To be successful in protecting your calling, follow the steps outlined in these past three chapters: Identify your weakness, put on the armor of God and establish the guardrails that will keep you far from sin.

Stick to what you need to do to flourish!

──────────────┤ GOING DEEPER ├──────────────

1. If you have not yet gone through the four steps listed in this chapter to help you establish guardrails, go ahead and do that now. Are you committed to implementing these guardrails?

2. Of the five indicators that you are getting too close to a boundary, did one or two stick out to you as a current struggle? What steps are you going to take to create distance between yourself and that boundary?

───────────────┤ CLOSING PRAYER ├───────────────

O Lord, please forgive me for the times I have known to put up a boundary and failed to do so. From this point on, I desire to be a person who stays far from the sin boundary by implementing guardrails I know to be needed in my life. Show me where I might do this in my life and give me conviction to always see them through. I want to guard my heart, and I pray You would help me to do so. I know I cannot walk this journey alone and be above reproach without Your strength. I need You. Always and forever. Amen.

RECOVERING FROM THE MYTH

11

What If?

God rescued us from dead-end alleys and dark dungeons.
He's set us up in the kingdom of the Son he loves so much,
the Son who got us out of the pit we were in, got rid of
the sins we were doomed to keep repeating.

Colossians 1:13–14 MESSAGE

You might be reading this book and thinking, *These are great precautions, but what if I already messed up? What if I already crossed something off the untouchable list and made an epic fail?* And perhaps you are wondering if a second chance is possible—if redemption is possible.

Well, guess what? *Redemption is definitely possible!*

You are not too far gone, friend. You have incredible purpose and value even if you have made a mess of things.

I can relate to any doubts you might have about your value in the Kingdom of God. When I had sex outside of marriage and lost almost everything I held dear in life, I thought for sure God was done with me. For a while all I could see was my sin and shame, and from that perspective, complete redemption did not seem likely. God had given me incredible opportunities, and I had squandered them. Why would He trust me with anything of value again?

You are not alone in your feelings, should you feel this way. I have been there, as have thousands of other believers, I am sure. I mean, look at the great cloud of witnesses who surround us. Hebrews 11 lists some mighty men and women of God who were commended for their faith. Yet many of them had their own epic fails. The list includes people guilty of murder, lying, prostitution, deception, adultery and more. It is a great example that you can make a mistake and still be used in great ways.

You are not alone, and you can find redemption. But to find redemption you will have to start with confession. Without confession, redemption is not possible. So before you do anything else, if you have not yet confessed your sins to God, pull away now and do that. Go to the Father on your knees and in whole submission, with full sorrow for what you have done, and ask Him for forgiveness. If you genuinely ask, He will fully give it.

Once you ask God for forgiveness, forgive yourself. Extend some grace to *you*! You might have a tendency to be hard on yourself, but if God can forgive you, then *you* can forgive you. It is time to stop carrying the baggage and live in the freedom God has extended to you!

Do you think you can do that—extend a little grace to yourself?

As you go through this process, you will certainly have to sift through a myriad of emotions—feelings of shame, guilt, condemnation and discouragement—just as David had to do:

"Why are you cast down, O my soul, and why are you in turmoil within me? Hope in God; for I shall again praise him, my salvation and my God" (Psalm 42:5–6).

David is in one of these seasons in Psalm 42. Though this song is attributed to the sons of Korah, musicians appointed by David to serve in the Tabernacle, most commentators agree that David is the likely author. And in all honesty, he is depressed. He is in exile, on the run, in hiding and mourning what has been left behind. Can you imagine being driven from your home, away from your family, with people looking to harm you? I cannot! It was a very hard season for David, and we get a glimpse of it as he shares with great vulnerability what he is going through.

It is easy when going through a hard time to get caught up in the emotions and sit in the unlovely. The trouble with sitting in the unlovely is that your view becomes narrow and hope begins to diminish. It focuses on what is going wrong and not on what God can do.

That is why David gets ahold of himself here. He knows that sitting in the unlovely will do him no good and, furthermore, that hope in God is a much better place to sit in.

When you are downcast and sad, perhaps depressed, it is important that you get ahold of yourself. David begins to talk to himself, asking his soul why it is downcast. Why are you downcast when you know God will act? He will move. That is cause for hope!

When you are in your hard seasons, it is okay to be sad or to struggle with what is going on. But there comes a point—and it can happen even while you are sad—that you begin to remind yourself of who God is. Remember when He has shown up for you before, and encourage yourself with the hope that He will show up for you again. God is the same yesterday, today and tomorrow, which means that if He has been there for you in the past, He will be there for you always.

Hope is powerful. Hope can keep you going. Hope can get you through the season. Hope acts in faith—faith that God is who He says He is and will be the good Father who takes good care of His children. A good parent—and indeed our God is—does not forsake his children. God might seem silent at times, but He is *always* there.

The first step in moving forward into redemption is to confess your sins to God and then forgive yourself. As you go through these steps and continue to move forward into redemption, keep control over your emotions. If you let them run free, you could be lost in depression, shame and, perhaps, even continue to sin. There is nothing like immense pain to drive you to a dark place, so get ahold of your emotions before they get ahold of you.

A Story of Redemption

One of my favorite stories of redemption in the Bible is that of Ruth. The book of Ruth opens with the story of a family living in Bethlehem—a man named Elimelech; his wife, Naomi; and their two sons, Mahlon and Chilion. They were living in a town known as "the house of bread," yet they were facing a time of famine during the reign of the judges. The writer does not tell us much about the circumstances of the family; we begin almost immediately with them traveling to the land of Moab.

Now for the record, God never told the family to go to Moab. It is likely Elimelech did not trust God to provide for his family during the famine or to bring them through the difficult season. So out of his own limited understanding, he uprooted his family and took them to a wicked nation. While living in

Moab, each son took a Moabite woman as his wife, and one of those women was named Ruth. Good thing God uses our poor choices for a bigger picture!

Naomi eventually lost her husband and both sons, leaving her a widow with two also-widowed daughters-in-law. After her devastating loss, she decided to return home to Bethlehem, and Ruth went with her.

Now, being from Moab was frowned upon in Bethlehem. Ruth's people were not favorites of the Israelites, let's just say. Not only was she a foreigner in a minority that was looked down upon, but she was also a widow who had faced much loss. Tack on her likely fear of living in a new place, working the lowly position of gleaning in the fields with the poor and being uncertain of her future, and you have a woman in much need of redemption.

But guess what? Her story did not end there! God was working behind the scenes to weave a beautiful story of redemption. A story that would include marriage to a godly man and a position in the lineage of the Messiah!

Ruth's Road to Redemption

In her journey to redemption, God took Ruth along the paths of grace, restoration, healing and purpose.

Grace

We see the path of grace opening for Ruth when God brought her out of Moab, out of her past and out of her loss. Did she deserve what He was doing in her life or what He was about to do? No. But we serve a God who loves the undeserving.

Grace is receiving what we do not deserve—the unmerited favor of God. It is getting all the good gifts we have been given in life. If we are honest with ourselves, we have to realize that we do not deserve any good thing—not even our salvation. But God loves us so much! He is a good Father who longs to bless His children. Jesus said, "If you then, who are evil, know how to give good gifts to your children, how much more will your Father who is in heaven give good things to those who ask him!" (Matthew 7:11).

John 3:16 tells us the great lengths God went to for us. He sent His own Son to this earth to die for you and me: "For God so loved the world, that he gave his only Son, that whoever believes in him should not perish but have eternal life." What else will He not do for you?

Isaiah 1:18 (MESSAGE) tells us that, "If your sins are blood-red, they'll be snow-white. If they're red like crimson, they'll be like wool." Although your fallen nature covered you in a cloak stained with uncleanliness, at your salvation God's grace made you pure. Truly! In God's eyes you are justified, just as if the sin never happened at all.

In this process, God made you a new creation: "Therefore, if anyone is in Christ, the new creation has come: The old has gone, the new is here!" (2 Corinthians 5:17 NIV).

In Jesus Christ you are a new person. This does not mean that you will never make mistakes. It does not mean that you never need to tell God you are sorry. But it does mean that you are not the moral failure, lie, rebellion or mistake you have made. You are new, redeemed, restored and clean.

Through His grace extended to Ruth, God shows you that your past does not define you. Yes, it will shape you, determine some consequences and potentially cause some future obstacles.

I faced church correction and took a step back as a result of my sin, but it was necessary and beneficial to my moving forward. Confronting my actions, although difficult, allowed me to move forward.

I want to make one thing abundantly clear: *Your past will never trump God's vision of who you are or where you are going.* He will use it!

Restoration

In addition to walking the path of grace, Ruth experienced restoration. Have you ever heard the phrase, "Leave it better than you found it"?

My parents still live in the same three-story house in Missouri that I grew up in. It is an old house that has not been updated much. A few years ago, it still had those dark accents, floral wallpaper and dated fixtures reminiscent of the '60s. My parents decided to spend a month in Florida for their anniversary around that time, so my three brothers and I decided it would be fun to do some updating on the main floor while they were gone. Some fresh paint on the walls, updated décor and even a new toilet installed by yours truly. (Boy, was that harder and more disgusting than I thought!)

We wanted my parents to come home to a different house—a better house. You see, I mentioned earlier how we siblings would fight. Over the years we had made a bit of a mess of the place, including broken doors and holes in the walls. We wanted to make good on the destruction we had caused and leave the house better than we had left it. Not sure if the fresh paint, updated décor and new toilet did the trick, but I like to think it looks a bit nicer! And our parents were really pleased.

God is in the business of making us better through restoration. He might find you tattered and broken in the aftermath of your sin, but He will not leave you there—He will go to work and leave you better than He found you.

God takes the broken and restores. The guilty and forgives. The ashamed and gives hope. He fills emptiness with purpose. This is what Jesus wants to do in your life. He wants to take a tattered and broken person and make you better than ever before. When Jesus goes to work on us we become unrecognizable to the people who knew us before. Any time I share my story of how I used to be in bondage to anger, people find it hard to believe I was once filled with rage. I tell them every time that the change was possible only because of God's handiwork and grace. That is the power of restoration.

Furthermore, God's definition of *restoration* does not mean just putting us back together; it means going above and beyond in making us better than before. We are always in far better shape after Jesus has gone to work in us than before. It does not mean we will not suffer or feel the growing pains because we will, but here is our promise:

> The suffering won't last forever. It won't be long before this generous God who has great plans for us in Christ—eternal and glorious plans they are!—will have you put together and on your feet for good. He gets the last word; yes, he does.

These lines from 1 Peter 5:10–11 (MESSAGE) explain that we will suffer, but God will restore us. That is not "maybe" or "if He feels like it." That is a promise. God will restore His people to a better place.

For Ruth this meant that she was no longer an outsider, alone and poor in Bethlehem. Through her marriage to Boaz she had family and purpose beyond anything she could have hoped for!

You might feel as though your past has left you too broken to be of any use. You might feel so used and ashamed that you are convinced God could never use someone like you. But these are lies the enemy wants you to believe to keep you down so that you never fulfill God's purpose for your life. Rebuke those thoughts, and remind yourself of these Scriptures we are learning regarding your future.

Healing

Ruth also experienced healing on her path to redemption. After all of her loss and pain, she was blessed not only with a godly husband and the security of a home, but she gave birth to a son. We sometimes think that when God puts us back together, it looks like the pieces of a broken vase being fitted and glued into place. There is more to it than this. God does internal work in your heart and soul that is healing as well. He heals you internally from the brokenness, guilt, sorrow and pain. He wants to reach down into the innermost parts of your heart and soul, where no one else can go, in order to mend and fill you with grace. To rid you of shame, guilt, sorrow, pain, insecurity. What is more, these are works only God can do; no human has the ability to reach the depths of the heart and soul and fill the void.

I mentioned early in this book that when I hit rock bottom and lived in a dark place for many months, I tried the world's way of "healing." I was trying to bypass the time proper healing required with a quick fix. I soon discovered that there was no way healing was possible by the world's means. Instead, I found my path to healing in Jeremiah 30.

Let's read two verses from this chapter that set the stage: "For thus says the Lord: Your hurt is incurable, and your wound is grievous" (Jeremiah 30:12); "for I will restore health to you, and your wounds I will heal, declares the Lord" (Jeremiah 30:17).

At first these verses seem to contradict themselves. Verse 12 claims that our hurts are incurable and our wounds grievous. Yet, five verses later we read that health can be restored and wounds can be healed! How can pain and wounds be incurable in one breath and healed in the next? The understanding lies in the context.

Wounds cannot heal when that healing is sought in the world. It is impossible. But with God any wound can be healed. The difference lies in the source. I saw hope for what I thought was incurable and placed my trust in the God who heals.

Dealing with the pain and brokenness face to face was not easy. As I opened up the Word of God and began poring over Scripture, however, I learned that it is not promised to be. Few things are more challenging than recovering from a broken heart, lost dream or grievous situation. In the darkest storms the hope of healing is the only light that has the power to pierce through, like a ray of sunshine parting the thick clouds. For us as Christians, we know that the hope Christ provides is our only way of survival.

How do you weather the storm? How do you, when all seems lost, persevere till you enter into that light at the end of the tunnel? It is important to understand what Scripture says about finding hope for personal healing, whether it be physical, emotional or spiritual. Because if you are not careful, you will pursue healing in an unhealthy or worldly way and completely bypass proper healing, as I tried to do.

The truth is, without God complete healing is not possible. Only Christ and the Word of God have the ability to reach those broken and achy places within our souls. What path will you choose; where will you pursue healing? What you choose to allow in will determine the process and completion of your healing.

Remember, there is no bypass to proper healing.

So, how do you pursue proper healing? Speaking from personal experience, I found a few things to be quite helpful. To a woman who felt all dried up on the inside, no verses brought life back into my bones more than those in Hosea 2. It's this beautiful and dramatic portrayal of Israel's journey from hardship to restoration. But it also parallels our own situations so powerfully.

"Therefore, behold, I will allure her, and bring her into the wilderness and speak tenderly to her. And there I will give her her vineyards and make the Valley of Achor [trouble] a door of hope. And there she shall answer as in the days of her youth, as at the time when she came out of the land of Egypt. And in that day, declares the Lord, you will call me 'My Husband,' and no longer will you call me 'My Baal.' For I will remove the names of the Baals from her mouth, and they shall be remembered by name no more. And I will make for them a covenant on that day with the beasts of the field, the birds of the heavens, and the creeping things of the ground. And I will abolish the bow, the sword, and war from the land, and I will make you lie down in safety. And I will betroth you to me forever. I will betroth you to me in righteousness and in justice, in steadfast love and in mercy. I will betroth you to me in faithfulness. And you shall know the LORD.

"And in that day I will answer, declares the LORD, I will answer the heavens, and they shall answer the earth, and the earth shall answer the grain, the wine, and the oil, and they shall answer Jezreel, and I will sow her for myself in the land. And I will have mercy on No Mercy, and I will say to Not My People, 'You are my people'; and he shall say, 'You are my God.'"

Hosea 2:14–23

Beginning in verse 14, there is this wooing of Israel where God wants to bring His children close to Him on a personal level. Then it describes how, although we may currently be in a Valley of Achor (also known as "Valley of Trouble"), there is a door of hope in the future.

Essentially, God wants to bring you close to Him and, there in your valley of trouble and pain, show you there is this hope before you. That the trouble won't last forever.

Further in verse 16, there is a transition between the levels of relationship. Again noting a more personal level, God wants you to see Him no longer as just a master, but as a "Husband." This reiterates affection toward His people. We then see a key phrase mentioned three times in two verses, "I will betroth you." When a phrase or word is mentioned multiple times in a short passage, it means it is very important to understand what is being said. God wants to make sure we know the importance of His covenant and restoring love.

The chapter leaves us with a confirmation by letting us know He will show love to us, even if we may feel unloved. To a woman who felt really lonely and unloved after a heart-wrenching loss, nothing made me feel more comforted than those words.

In your grief and pain, coming face to face with the circumstances won't be easy. However, it will be worth it, and I want to help if I can. Which is why I want to talk through a blueprint to proper healing.

I happened to come across a powerful account in 2 Samuel 12 after I had committed to the healing process, and it was a game changer for me. In this deeply sorrowful account, King David has just lost the son his wife Bathsheba had given birth to. He lost the son because of the sins he had committed, both in having an affair with Bathsheba and then having her husband killed to cover up the scandal. So, on top of having the weight of guilt from such devastating sin, he loses his precious child.

Most would say that losing a child is by far one of the hardest things a person could go through. Maybe you are personally experiencing such grief now? The loss of someone we love is hard to manage whether that is through death, divorce or breakup.

What David did after his child died is remarkable and truly an example for us in our healing process. Scripture shows that the first thing David did was worship God. In fact, it is such a hard act to comprehend that David is questioned for doing it. So why did he? David understood he couldn't change what happened, but he could choose how to respond. David knew that above all else, God was good no matter the season and that the focus must be on Him, not on the circumstances.

As I pored over these words in my season of grief, I asked myself an important question.

"If David could worship in his grief of losing a child, couldn't I worship at the ruins of a relationship?"

Shouldn't my appropriate response be to seek after God with all my heart, even out of the depths of my pain? So I worshiped and found that as I did, the grief lifted and comfort abounded.

As hard as it might feel to be thankful, it is necessary. In fact, as soon as you are done reading this, I hope you will turn on some worship music, begin seeking God and worship the One who has saved you from an eternity of constant sorrow.

Worship is key to the healing process because it takes the focus off your situation and onto your faithful God. Once I began worshiping and focusing less on my grief, I was able to start implementing other things. In Romans 12 we see the attributes of a true Christian, and indeed they should be represented even in our grief; however, there are a few that are particularly helpful in such a season.

Rejoicing in hope. Patience in tribulation. Being constant in prayer. Those three consistencies in the storm will guide you through to the other side. Again, these are not necessarily easy when you are struggling to get through the day; however, they are a part of the healing process. More specifically, they provide the right perspective to see the end game.

Rejoicing in hope means recognizing that Christ will return and we can celebrate an eternity with Him. So even though it is rough now, it is only temporary compared to the everlasting state of our souls. As a result, we can be patient through the tribulation and above all, pray through it.

You see, prayer changes things. My youth pastor used to say that the battle is won in prayer. So if the battle for your healing rests in the consistency of your prayers, pray often. Go forth today with a commitment to be grateful for your eternal destination, patience to see through the storm and constant in your prayers.

The final stretch of your journey to proper healing will require perseverance.

Hebrews 10:35–36 (NLT) is one of my favorite verses in the Bible and says this:

So do not throw away this confident trust in the Lord. Remember the great reward it brings you! Patient endurance is what you need now, so that you will continue to do God's will. Then you will receive all that he has promised.

Healing came slow those long months, and I know that is not the most encouraging thing to hear. But things did change when I committed to the healing process God's way instead of shortcutting my way out. It will take time, but that is where the message of Hebrews 10 steps in for encouragement. It is one of my favorite verses and has sustained me through some pretty challenging seasons in life.

Perseverance is a must-have on the journey to complete healing. It means getting out of bed in the morning, going to work and making it through the day, one day at a time. It means doing those things you don't feel like doing, like worship and prayer. Perseverance is trusting that God has a purpose for you and will be with you. If you can persevere through the grief and pain, you will come out on the other end with a great reward. You will be more mature, abundant in faith and better equipped to minister to others out of your own story. Furthermore, you will receive an eternal reward that cannot be bought with the shortcuts of this world.

As someone who pursued healing from this world, I can tell you it does not work. Some things may mask the pain temporarily, but they will never allow you to heal. Only God can, and I hope you will pursue the road less traveled for the only healing that will restore you. Make a commitment each day to pursue God's way of healing, which reaches the depths of your soul and replaces the pain with peace.

Purpose

Ruth's final stop on her journey to redemption was that of purpose. The Bible tells us that she was a mother in the family line of David. After grace, restoration and healing take place in your life, God propels you into your purpose. It may be slow, but it is worth it!

Ruth knew long-suffering and could have given up; she faced many bumps in the road. Enduring those bumps and allowing God to take her on a journey to redemption resulted in being part of the lineage of Christ! She was not too far gone, and neither are you.

Broken can be restored. Sorrow can be turned into joy. Empty can be made full. Worthless can be valued. Not good enough can be recast. Isaiah 61:3 (NIV) paints a beautiful picture of redemption:

> To bestow on them a crown of beauty instead of ashes, the oil of joy instead of mourning, and a garment of praise instead of a spirit of despair. They will be called oaks of righteousness, a planting of the LORD for the display of his splendor.

There is nothing more valuable in this universe to God than His children—and that includes you! God has a plan for you regardless of your past choices, upbringing and culture. God sees His child when He looks at you, and He sees value. With value comes purpose.

Your purpose and dreams matter to God. He has put something in you to be birthed; a seed of sorts to be nurtured through your pain and long-suffering in order to spring forth at a very specific time. Continuing in sin will only lead you down a dead-end road; you must turn from it to let God lead you through the process of grace, restoration, healing and purpose.

Pursue the path of redemption and anything is possible.

Feeling like a Failure

Along the journey there will be times you feel like a failure. Those emotions are incredibly hard to live with. I will be honest; I have been feeling a bit of that lately. I shared my story with you about going into the ICU on the heels of my son's birth and, through a series of events, ending up feeling like a total failure as a mom and wife. Professionally, I have had a few things change for me over the last year that have left me feeling discouraged. No matter the circumstances, whether the failure is from a choice you make or something that happens beyond your control, failure is failure—and it is plain awful!

I know what it is like to feel you are not good enough. To feel you have messed up beyond repair. To believe that you have no value or worth. To be overlooked even though you have worked hard with passion and integrity. To be criticized and bullied. These feelings are painful and cut to the very core of your being.

If you are feeling anything similar at all and label yourself a failure, please know that you are not. Yes, maybe you did mess up. But God's restorative power is far more capable of labeling you *Redeemed* than anything else is to label you *Failure*.

So what can you do when you feel like a failure? When you feel discouraged by emotions of shame and guilt? As we saw earlier, David gives us a great example in Psalm 42, encouraging us to get ahold of the inner man—to capture those thoughts and feelings. Once you have done so, here are four steps you can take to move outside of failure:

1. Remind yourself that God's mercies are new every day (see Lamentations 3:22–23). Maybe you made a mistake or messed up yesterday. Guess what? Today is a brand-new day, and Scripture illustrates the beauty of a new day. God wants to extend to you a gift of a new beginning and forgiveness. He wants you to embrace this gift today and every day.

2. Know that God uses every wrong decision and mistake for His glory (see Jeremiah 29:11). Everything in your life is woven together for a much bigger plan, and nothing you do will surprise God. He considers every misstep and bad decision along the way, never allowing it to throw off His plans for you. God wants to use you even with all your epic fails.

3. Remember that His strength is made perfect in your weakness (see 2 Corinthians 12:9). I have said this a dozen times already, but it is that important! Embrace your areas of weakness, because God's strength can show up there and He will be glorified.

4. Cast your cares on Him (see Psalm 55:22). Whatever fear, worry or anxiety you are carrying, you do not have to carry it alone. God has some mighty shoulders to lean on. Cast your burdens and concerns on Him, and He will help carry those cares for you.

These are all steps I have actively taken lately. I know they work, so move forward yourself, friend. You no longer have to live with those heavy emotions of failure and discouragement. No one can flourish in such a state of mind. Shake it off and step into redemption.

Redemption Is Possible

How are your "what ifs" doing now in the light of redemption? Have I made a good case that redemption is possible for you? If there is still any doubt in your mind, remember what Jesus did for you.

The Son of God did not have to come to earth. He did not have to wrap Himself in flesh and live as a man for 33 years. And He certainly did not have to die. But He did . . . all of it. And you know why He did it? For you. Yes, you! He would have done it all if it were just for you.

Jesus paid the ultimate price when He sacrificed Himself on the cross. He took all your sins upon Himself and died the death of a sinner. Thank goodness He is who He says He is, because He was able to conquer death—something only He could do. And through that victory, you have only to ask Jesus to be your Lord and Savior in order to be granted access to your loving Father.

Jesus paid the price for you. He extends His victory to you. And not just once at salvation but every day. When you mess up, no matter how big, know that there is a gift waiting to be received by you each and every day. Never let it go.

Take in the words of Colossians 1:13–14 (MESSAGE) and allow them to soothe your tattered heart and hurting soul:

God rescued us from dead-end alleys and dark dungeons. He's set us up in the kingdom of the Son he loves so much, the Son who got us out of the pit we were in, got rid of the sins we were doomed to keep repeating.

God is a rescuer of hearts, no matter where those hearts might be hiding. He is captivated by you and wants nothing more than to be in an intimate relationship with you. This is why the Father gave up His Son, why Jesus laid down His life on the cross: so that *you* could be rescued out of those dead-end alleys and dark dungeons.

He wants to break the cycle—your cycle of sin and pain. Will you allow Him? You can start today on a new path, a path worthy of the calling placed on your life, filled with great purpose for the Kingdom.

Confess your sins. Forgive yourself. And take the path of redemption to a life that glorifies God.

─────────────────┤ GOING DEEPER ├─────────────────

1. Are you struggling to find redemption in the aftermath of sin? How has the story of Ruth shaped your perspective? Perhaps take some time to journal what God is tenderly speaking to your heart regarding the possibility of redemption!

2. Of the four steps listed to help you move past feeling like a failure, which speaks most powerfully to you and why?

---| CLOSING PRAYER |---

Father, I am so sorry for taking decisions into my own hands and recklessly attempting to do life on my own. Will You please forgive me? And help me to forgive myself? I don't want to live in condemnation and listen to the enemy's attempts to hold me in fear. I long to live in the freedom You offer without shame. Guide me on this journey to redemption. Show me how to embrace grace and be an example to others of what restoration can look like. Thank You, again. Amen.

12

Moving Forward

> "Forget the former things; do not dwell on the past. See, I am doing a new thing! Now it springs up; do you not perceive it? I am making a way in the wilderness and streams in the wasteland."
>
> Isaiah 43:18–19 NIV

Remember: Your past will never trump God's vision of who you are or where you are going. With that in mind, you can move forward into a flourishing life that radiates the love and goodness of God.

In the last chapter, those of us with "what ifs" and past failures got to take a dive into redemption. Now with a foundation in place to begin anew, it is time for all of us to take the practical steps we discovered in "Part 3: The Death of the Myth." Having found redemption, first you must admit weakness. In admitting weakness, God's strength is made perfect, and you will have

Him with you in any temptation. Next, make a choice each day to put on the armor of God, and then establish guardrails.

These are steps you must take to overcome an untouchable mindset. This might require some hard work on your part, but it will enable you to have victory over temptation. Are you ready to commit to doing what is necessary to flourish in life, even if it is hard? As we close, I want to stress a few critically important points that we have touched on.

Prepare for Every Possibility

If you are truly committed to moving forward in this journey to overcome an untouchable mindset, you should prepare for every possibility. If there is any situation you find yourself in that could be a haunt from the past or cause you to stumble given the right circumstances, you must prepare ahead of time for how you will handle the situation—because anyone can commit any sin under the right conditions.

Let's look at a few examples of how to prepare for a possibility.

If your father was an alcoholic who set an example of turning to the bottle to deal with stress, you might be prone to addiction, particularly alcohol. In this case it might be beneficial to refrain from drinking alcohol at all, even in social situations. This will remove the temptation to form a dependency on alcohol.

If you are married you must have boundaries with people of the opposite sex. I once worked with a pastor who would copy his wife on all email with the opposite sex for accountability. Mad respect for that guy!

Remember the woman who had an affair with a man she rode in the car with? Not a good idea to be alone with someone of the opposite sex, or to share emotions and feelings that foster intimacy. It is not about how close you can get to temptation but how to be above reproach.

If you are responsible for finances within your company, include someone else in your financial decisions and share all records with transparency. You might not imagine that you would ever steal, but, again, under the right circumstances the pressure can be just enough to be a tipping point into sin. I once heard a story of someone whose close family member became ill, and under that pressure she stole from her employer to pay for the medical bills.

Maybe you are dating someone—I have some good insight here. Simply do not be alone with the person you are dating if temptation could at all lead to sin. Maybe you should not kiss or lie next to each other while watching a movie. When Ryan and I started dating again, we did not kiss for five months. Five months! If you have ever dated someone you deeply care about, you know how hard that is. But it was something we knew we needed to do to stay on the right track. Think what would be most helpful to you and be willing to make the hard decisions in dating in order to have a healthy relationship long term.

I want to be clear for a moment. I am not here to push a bunch of rules on you or to overwhelm you with legality. I am simply suggesting that in order to be victorious over any temptation, you must be willing to make some choices that could be hard or inconvenient. Would you rather make momentary sacrifices in order to be free from long-term shame and regret? It will always be worth it in the long run.

Prepare for any and every possibility before it even becomes an option.

Never Give Up

You, dear friend, have a powerful tool in your possession now: the knowledge that will allow you to be victorious in many situations. That does not mean there will be no hiccups or mistakes along the way. The important thing to remember is: Never give up! You can keep pressing forward on the path God has placed you on regardless of what you have been through.

Preston is a man who knows redemption is possible. He grew up in the Catholic Church and followed all the rules from a young age. When he was eight years old, he woke up one morning and knew he was supposed to be in ministry. At the age of thirteen, he woke up and felt confident he was supposed to go into vocational ministry. Once again, when he was eighteen years old, he woke up one morning and the same thing happened to him.

Although he believed ministry was his path, Preston chose to go to college to pursue engineering out of an interest in math and science. It was there, during his freshman year, that his life took a turn.

At first Preston attended a new, vibrant nondenominational church near the school. It was not the Catholic service he was used to, but it piqued his interest. After eight months of attending church, Preston stopped all of a sudden. His Sundays started to look different. Instead, he began going over to his girlfriend's house at her request; she wanted nothing to do with church.

Preston and his girlfriend eventually moved in together. At that point, he was feeling far away from God and could tell the difference in his life. One day out of the blue, Preston felt that God was telling him to go to a young adults' retreat being hosted by the nondenominational church he had once attended;

he remembered they often had them. In reality, Preston had no idea there was a retreat; God was speaking to him and calling him back. But guess what? Preston returned to the church that Sunday—the last day to sign up for a retreat! Don't you love how God works!

Preston attended the retreat and came out of that weekend with a renewed interest in attending church. When he told his girlfriend about his desire to go back, she declined to go. Within a month Preston broke up with her because he wanted to go in a direction she had no interest in.

Instead of diving into faith as he had hoped, however, Preston fell into depression as a result of losing someone he cared about. In that lonely place he became bitter toward the church—even though he knew his struggles were his own doing.

Over the next two years Preston stayed away from church. He went on to attend school in Australia, where his closest friend was a Christian. Upon returning to the United States, the only place he could find to live was with an old friend who used to go to church with him. God was working to bring Preston back!

His friend began inviting him to the church they once attended. Preston turned him down time and again; he had no interest in returning. One day, however, his roommate grabbed his arm and fairly dragged him to the young adults' service at the church. The next week, the same thing. And it was that second night that flipped a switch for Preston. He recommitted his life to God. He chose to make Christ first.

Preston went on to have a career in engineering, but God spoke to his heart once again about going into full-time ministry. Today, Preston is working for that same young adults' ministry that had such a huge impact on him. He is pointing people to

God who are at a stage in life that is much like the one he was in when his life forever changed.

Remember: You are surrounded by a great cloud of witnesses; people in the Bible who had their own epic fails yet whom God used in tremendous ways. The liar who fathered the nation of God. The murderer who led Israel out of captivity. The adulterer who ruled over God's people. The Pharisee who murdered Christians but eventually became one of the most influential people in the early Church, wrote much of the New Testament and served as the first missionary to the Gentiles. These are just a few of the powerful stories of redemption we find in the Bible.

There are also people all around you struggling with similar temptations. When I had sex outside of marriage, I thought I was the only Christian girl in southwest Missouri who had made that mistake. When many young Christians began sharing with me similar experiences, though, I realized I was not alone. There is a real struggle being faced and battle being waged; we can be strong together through accountability and encouragement.

You are not alone. Beyond knowing that you are not the only one to make an epic fail of your kind, tap into your support system for encouragement. Lean on the godly people in your life who can walk through this journey with you. Ecclesiastes 4:9–10 illustrates the importance of relationships so well: "Two are better than one, because they have a good reward for their toil. For if they fall, one will lift up his fellow. But woe to him who is alone when he falls and has not another to lift him up!"

You do not have to do life alone. Walk through it with the people God has placed in your life. Godly relationships are important in this journey and vital to navigating the ups and downs. In the downs, there is someone there to lift you up.

And finally, always and above all, lean on Jesus. This is the most important thing you can do each day.

Weakness Is Strength

These are our final moments left together on this redemptive journey. I have shared with you, transparently and vulnerably, things I have never spoken about outside of my marriage in the hopes that it creates a connection between us and serves as a cautionary word. My experience of moral failure brought to the surface the untouchable myth and its ability to cause anyone who is unguarded to fall.

I hope you have gathered from this book how to identify the untouchable myth and where you might be struggling with this in your own life. In addition to identifying it, I pray you have learned how to overcome it. You can be victorious over this area and in all areas through the power of Christ, who overcame death and extends that same victory to you in your everyday life.

Are you ready and willing to go there—to go to that place of vulnerability? Remember, this is key: It starts by admitting your weakness. Once you have done that, you can find strength—strength from God that is made perfect in your weakness. Tap into that place, and you will find an incredible ability to stand firm against the untouchable myth.

You can do this. You can overcome. Be the shining example of a life surrendered to Christ and flourishing in the freedom of weakness tied to strength in a harmonious relationship.

Moving Forward

Isaiah 43 has often reminded me, in the midst of my biggest failures and greatest struggles, that I am not alone. I am not my past. And neither are you. God wants you to take those former thoughts, actions and motives, and forget them. Leave them in the past. Leave them where they belong because He is doing a new thing in your life—today! He is making a way out of the wilderness and streams in the wasteland. He is producing life and life-giving fruit in your new life, apart from the past.

Do you want to embrace this new way, this new life? Then stop going over old history and take notice of what God is doing in your life *today*! He is bringing you into a new and a vibrant life:

> "Forget about what's happened; don't keep going over old history. Be alert, be present. I'm about to do something brand-new. It's bursting out! Don't you see it? There it is! I'm making a road through the desert, rivers in the badlands."
>
> Isaiah 43:18–19 MESSAGE

―――――――――| GOING DEEPER |―――――――――

1. As you near the end of this journey to freedom from the untouchable myth, what has stuck out most to you in this book? Where do you feel God challenging you the most?
2. How will your life look different after this book? Having the tools and knowing you can flourish by admitting weakness, what do you need to start doing differently?

——————————————| CLOSING PRAYER |——————————————

God, I thank You that my story does not end with the sin. That You restore me and use me even though I have messed up in the past. I commit to follow You wholeheartedly all the days of my life and to lean into You for the strength to do so. Help me to take what I have learned in this book and apply it faithfully. Above all, be magnified and glorified in my life. It is You who deserves all the glory and the honor and the praise. Amen!

Afterword

Confronting Sin

> Brothers and sisters, if a person is discovered in some sin,
> you who are spiritual restore such a person in a spirit of
> gentleness.
>
> Galatians 6:1 NET

I would be doing an injustice if I spent so much time talking about church discipline without addressing this hot topic. This book has thus far spoken to those who find themselves on the side of making epic fails. But what if you are the one having to confront the sin? Or what if you have heard the phrase *church discipline* and recoil with disbelief that a church would do that to anyone? So before we end this journey together, I want to address two topics: the often-misunderstood practice of church discipline, and how someone (perhaps even you at some point) should respond to a person who has sinned.

Church Discipline

Many who hear the two words *church discipline* fear the idea of it or have themselves experienced some bad form of it. Either way, church discipline is not meant to be an archaic practice that scares believers. In fact, if done in a healthy and loving way, church discipline is a beautiful thing. Let me explain.

Church discipline is reserved for two situations. The first is when a member of a church or fellowship resists correction from two or three people who have witnessed the person's sin. This process is outlined in Matthew 18, and we discuss it below. The second is confronting a leader in a church who needs to be held accountable.

Both situations must be handled with absolute truth—but also with grace and love. Without grace and love in the equation, church discipline will leave wounds and cause disunity in the Body.

Consider the dynamics of a parent/child relationship; discipline is part of a loving corrective process to help the child mature and grow into a well-rounded person. No good parents love to discipline their children; however, out of love, they do it for the child's ultimate good.

Our heavenly Father does the same for His children—us. He corrects us when we sin and restores us lovingly if we humble ourselves. Discipline has a heavy and fearful sound to it for those who have experienced it done incorrectly, which is many. If done right, however, it can be exactly what a person needs to be directed down a good path and to grow into the person God envisions him or her to be. It is designed to bring people back into relationship with God and His Church; it is a loving act of brotherhood and sisterhood, with everyone coming around the broken person in love and grace.

Galatians 6:1 (NET) says, "Brothers and sisters, if a person is discovered in some sin, you who are spiritual restore such a person in a spirit of gentleness." I am thankful I experienced it this way—in gentleness. It is quite possible that if my sin had not been dealt with in a healthy and godly way, I could have been hurt to the point of division. I could have become angry and bitter, distancing myself from God and the Body of Christ. Yet because I underwent godly church discipline, I continued to go to that church for many years and experienced incredible support and restoration.

Second Corinthians 2:5–8 tells us this:

> Now if anyone has caused pain, he has caused it not to me, but in some measure—not to put it too severely—to all of you. For such a one, this punishment by the majority is enough, so you should rather turn to forgive and comfort him, or he may be overwhelmed by excessive sorrow. So I beg you to reaffirm your love for him.

I am thankful I went through church discipline. It was incredibly hard—one of the hardest things I have ever been through—but through such repentance I found support from the church community around me and was able to work through what I had done in a healthy way. I truly do not think I would have walked through that valley and be where I am today without it. Restoration would not have been possible. Discipline is never easy—it is a fire of sorts. But if done the right way, it is a fire by which a person is refined.

I just want you to know that the words *church discipline* do not have to be scary. And it is not wrong for a church to do such a thing. In fact, it is very necessary in certain situations.

Sin cannot be allowed to simmer under the surface or be swept under the rug. Like yeast in a batch of dough, sin will work its way through the Body. It must be dealt with.

Discipline Regarding a Leader

Regarding dealing with pastors and other prominent church leaders who are caught in sin, 1 Timothy 5:19–20 (NLT) says this: "Do not listen to an accusation against an elder unless it is confirmed by two or three witnesses. Those who sin should be reprimanded in front of the whole church; this will serve as a strong warning to others."

Leaders are meant to be an example and, therefore, above reproach. They lead by example and show others how to live a life wholly submitted to Christ. But as they lead in godliness by example they must also be an example to how sin destroys. When temptation takes root in a pastor's heart and sin has entered into his or her life, greater discipline is required—discipline that serves as an example to the consequences of sin.

Church leaders are shepherds over their flocks. They are responsible for the care of the people they lead. If a leader falls into sin, it is necessary for that leader to confess and repent before them. It is an obligation they have to those in their care. It also serves as a cautionary tale and warns others to stay far from sin.

I had to go to the leadership team I worked with to confess my sin. Some pastors and senior leaders may have to go in front of the whole church for confession, which I have seen as well. In general, leaders are held to a higher standard due to a more public role and, thus, must be disciplined before the Body they serve.

Again, the discipline must be done in love, humility and grace. Without those conditions in place, the discipline will lack the purity required for genuine transformation to take place. But done right, church discipline can be a conduit to grace and redemption in the Body of Christ.

Discipline Regarding a Friend

Jesus' words in Matthew 18:15–17 give us a clear path for dealing with a friend or family member who is sinning against us. Church discipline might be needed as part of the process:

> "If your brother sins against you, go and tell him his fault, between you and him alone. If he listens to you, you have gained your brother. But if he does not listen, take one or two others along with you, that every charge may be established by the evidence of two or three witnesses. If he refuses to listen to them, tell it to the church. And if he refuses to listen even to the church, let him be to you as a Gentile and a tax collector."

There are four steps outlined in this passage that tell us how to deal with a matter of sin:

1. *Go to the person one on one.* If you see sin in a friend's or family member's life, go to that one. If you have a problem with someone, speak to him or her first. Talking it out as two people, honestly and in love, is by far the best first approach. You never know; you could be perceiving the situation incorrectly, or your friend might repent without having to take the matter any further.
2. *Bring another along.* If going to the person alone does not work to bring repentance or reconciliation, it is time to bring another into the mix who can act as further witness to the need for correction. But this is important: Make

sure it is a godly person who can be trusted, someone who knows both you and the person being approached. That witness can confirm what is going on and help the person being confronted to comprehend the sin or the wrong being done.

3. *Tell it to the church.* If neither the first nor second approach works, it is time to bring it to the church. Note: The assumption is that the church is a loving fellowship that will not bring a charge with impure motives.

4. *Separation.* If nothing works to bring repentance from the sinner, ties must be cut. This is not meant to be an unloving act but, rather, a separation from sin. You can still extend grace and love to the person, but, the fact is, if at this point the person's heart has not been softened, chances are it might never be. Better to create distance so that the sin is not like yeast that spreads throughout the Body.

If you see sin in another's life or if you are upset with someone who has hurt you, Matthew 18 is the solution. It is the process God has established, and you are not above it, no matter how right or justified you might feel to go another route. One of the quickest ways of causing division in the Body of Christ is by circumventing healthy conflict. I cannot tell you how many times I have watched someone discuss with one person the problem he or she has with another person instead of talking to the offending person directly.

You may feel you have the purest motives in telling an outside party, but that is not biblical and it is wrong. Matthew 18 tells you to go to that person if there is a fault; not a boss, not a pastor, not anyone else. Period. Bringing another into the situation takes place only when you have approached the person without resolution. You may then move to step two of the process, which is including someone else in the discussion who might help the individual turn from sin.

Would you want someone going to others and saying negative things about you? Would you want your name and character smeared? Of course not. So never do it to someone else. Always follow Jesus' words in Matthew 18 in a conflict.

Responding to a Person Who Has Sinned

Now, let's discuss the second topic about responding to a sinner. What if you learn that a friend or family member has sinned, perhaps even in a way you thought unimaginable? How do you interact with someone who has disappointed you, shocked you or done something a bit awkward and messy?

One of the things I noticed most after my moral failure was the way Christians were unsure of how to respond to me. During that period of my life, I had friends respond both graciously and not so graciously. I get it—you care about the person; but it is sin. So how do you respond?

From someone who has been on the receiving end of many responses, here are some tips I hope you will consider when responding to a person who is sinning or undergoing correction.

Be honest. A good friend is there for another, but a good friend also does not ignore sin. Ignoring it does not make it go away or help the heart condition of your friend.

Confrontation is never easy, but if done correctly, it can be one of the best things you could ever do for your friend. Remember always to follow Matthew 18 in the situation. It might be hard for your friend, but I promise that in the end confronting the sin is the best possible thing you can do.

Be gracious. Let me give you a bit of insight. True believers who fall into sin feel an incredible amount of shame and guilt. They probably feel a wedge between them and God as well. And they most likely feel as if other Christians will cast judgment their way should the scarlet letter be revealed.

Judgment never brings someone to repentance or healing. As a friend, you above all should be an extension of grace. Furthermore, you are a sinner, too, and yet God has extended incredible grace toward you. As a recipient of grace, you have no place to harbor judgment in your heart. In fact, those who have received the grace of God should be the greatest givers of it.

Be an extension of grace in your friend's life. Grace does not mean you are accepting the sin; it means you are looking past the sin to be there for a friend in need.

Be empathetic. If we are honest, we all have had—or have—something in our lives that is a stronghold or lingering sin. Pride, lying, drunkenness, judgment of others, gossip—something that our flesh has a struggle shaking loose from. You might not be able to relate to your friend's specific sin, but surely you can relate to the feeling of shame or guilt that accompanies sin.

When you have a friend in this dark and lonely place, you can be one of the greatest blessings by really being there. Really being there means extending empathy. Empathy is more than just feeling bad for someone; it is putting yourself in that person's shoes and feeling along with him or her. Put yourself in those shoes of guilt and really be there as a positive support system.

Be accountable. Making a commitment to refrain from sin and actually doing it are two different things. It may be hard for your friend to stay the course, at least for a while. Offer to provide some accountability. Meaning, if you know of some questionable circumstances or think there is a possibility for temptation, ask your friend how she or he is doing. People are less likely to do something wrong—or at least will think twice about it—if they know they will be asked about it.

I hope this provides some insight into how you can respond to a friend caught up in sin. Friendships are a blessing from the Lord, and these harder seasons can be great for fostering stronger believers and stronger friendships. This is not the time to see something messy and pull away; that is not what your friend needs. Forge through the messy, extend a little grace and choose to partner with your friend through restoration.

Discipline, sin and betrayal of trust are all messy and difficult situations to work through. There is, however, a godly and proper way to navigate it all. How you choose to walk through situations like this will be a major deciding factor in the longevity of your relationships.

I hope you can see through my experience and others' how confrontation and discipline can be a good thing: a redemptive act of love.

A Note from Ryan Rust

As a recently divorced 27-year-old, I was starting to gain my confidence back when I was invited to a friend's Easter lunch celebration. Indecisive, I finally agreed. Around this time in my life, I both craved and dreaded being with people. While social interactions were invigorating, I often left feeling exhausted. A friend once told me that people referred to me as Mr. Sad Eyes. I was not comfortable knowing that was how people saw me; I wanted to be happy again.

After church on Easter Sunday, I ran home, ironed my finest modern plaid shirt, dabbed on a little extra cologne and left Mr. Sad Eyes at home. The apartment was brimming with music, food and single people. One lady in particular grabbed my attention. She had fair skin, silk-black hair, emerald-green eyes and a relaxed disposition. She was beautiful! I floated over and introduced myself to her. Her name was Brett, no—Britt. Fumbling her name, I made a joke and recovered. I liked her and wanted to get to know her. But I was afraid. Afraid I would be rejected when she found out about my past.

Playing it safe, I found ways to meet up with Britt along with mutual friends. We enjoyed coffee, sushi, miniature golf and other fun things together that summer. My feelings for her grew, and I wanted to ask her out. Seeking advice from friends and family, I asked what people thought about me dating. Really, I was looking for validation. Some said, "Go for it; you deserve to be happy." Others advised that I needed more time to heal from the divorce. Tired of being sad, I assigned myself to the path that would invigorate my life again.

In my heart and mind I truly believed God would bless me for honoring Him. I attended church faithfully, read the Bible consistently, prayed and shared the power of Christ in my life. While I was not a perfect Christian, I was growing and pursuing Him wholeheartedly. Why would God not bless me with a favored life? I convinced myself.

Feeling entitled to a smart, beautiful and godly woman, I built up courage and asked Britt out. But first, I needed to do some damage control. I decided to come clean and address my past head on. I told her that I had been divorced—not once, but twice.

My throat tightened. Time slowed down.

She said yes to the date! Emotionally, I was moved by her grace and lack of judgment. Most people in my new circle of friends accepted me lovingly, but it still felt as though I was kept at arm's length. Tainted in some way. Britt's grace made me feel clean and affirmed.

As we dated I became more vulnerable—for the first time in a long time—and my emotional guardrails began to fall. The feelings of being desired and attractive gave me self-worth. I was happy again, and that is a powerful feeling.

During this time in my life, I was doing everything I could to become a God-honoring man. I was spiritually on fire for the

Lord and wanted my life to reflect that. Every week I attended a men's Bible study, a small group devotional and three to four church services. Plus I devoured nineteen different books, read through numerous books of the Bible and saw a Christian counselor. This regimen consumed my life, and it felt great.

God was blessing many areas of my life. The pain of my failed marriages was fading. Work was enjoyable. Prayers for myself and others were being answered more quickly than at any other time in my life. Spiritually I felt like Leonardo DiCaprio at the bow of the *Titanic*. I was in love with life, shielded by God's grace, covered in mercy and on course for a bright future. I felt untouchable.

While I was putting up many boundaries to defend against repeating history, I did not properly guard myself against my greatest vulnerability—validation from a woman. In my mind and heart I had no intention or plan to have sex. At the same time I had no plan to avoid the temptation of sex either. Because I was in a good place in my life, I assumed I was strong. Failing to acknowledge my vulnerability and guard myself, I fell short and succumbed to temptation. Britt and I had sex.

Immediately afterward I felt guilty. I did what I had vowed I would not do. *You big hypocrite*, I told myself. In one selfish act I dishonored not only Britt and myself but also all the great work God was doing in my life. It affected us both deeply, and I felt guilty.

A few days later Britt called. As she choked back tears it became clear she had something important to tell me. I feared she was pregnant.

Britt mumbled, "Can we talk?"

Now I was really freaking out! Then she told me she got fired from her coveted church position for having sex outside of marriage.

I was furious! Furious at everyone (but myself).

Bitterness began to grow in my heart for what I perceived to be cruel and unusual punishment. While devastated, Britt remained committed to church authority and willingly subjected herself to the process of church discipline. I could not understand why she did not just count her losses, walk away and move on. But her faith and commitment intrigued me.

Up to this point I had never witnessed church discipline or a church's willingness to restore a person. What was called restoration felt more like abuse, and I was vocal about that with Britt. Despite my feelings, Britt swallowed her pride, continued attending church and sought counsel.

In defiance I withdrew my heart from the fellowship and drifted into isolation for a time. The situation soon became a point of contention for Britt and me. I did not agree that she should be subjecting herself to such discipline. Because she was not angry in the same way I was angry, I began to pull away and eventually broke up with her. I was angry, bitter and wracked with guilt.

Months passed. Then one day Britt informed me that the church was holding a church discipline assembly instead of the usual church service.

"For *you*?" I asked, incredulous.

"No," Britt replied. Turns out, one of the pastors had come forward to confess he had had regular sexual relations with a prostitute.

That service was a defining moment for me because it began to change how I perceived the purpose of church discipline.

During the assembly the covering over of sin with love and grace was absolutely breathtaking. The offending pastor, completely broken by his sin, confessed tearfully with his equally broken yet faithful wife by his side. The lead pastor proceeded to explain that the purpose of church discipline is not about shunning or embarrassment. Rather, it is about bringing people back into right relationship with God and the church. He explained that perpetual sin in the church is like cancer. If one part is affected, the whole body suffers. You cannot ignore it and expect it to get better.

What I began to understand in that moment was that church discipline is intended to be administered with love. The lead pastor invited the church to forgive swiftly and openly and to embrace the offending pastor one by one with love and grace. The line took an hour. The act was beautiful. So beautiful, in fact, that something changed inside me.

Blinded by the stubbornness of my sin, I had failed to see that my anger and defiance were not only affecting me but also hurting Britt and the church. At the same moment, unspeakable love flooded me. Through that incredible display of love and grace, I understood God wanted me back. He wanted me reconnected to His Body.

By taking the path of least resistance and avoiding confrontation, I was actually binding myself to my sin through a refusal to repent. My relationship with the church suffered. I isolated myself from friends and pushed Britt away. That is what my sin did to me, and it is the same for you. Sin separates us from God and the Body.

Ultimately, I was refusing to repent. As a result I had been interpreting what was happening as abusive. With an unrepentant heart I had been inwardly accusing the church for being unloving and unfair. Because I withdrew from the church, it stunted my spiritual growth and cost me the woman I loved.

For me, understanding the biblical purpose of church discipline, i.e., loving restoration, changed my heart. Not only was this process intended for my restoration but also the purification of the Church. This was a big revelation for me—to see how individual sin affects others.

I valued happiness above obedience. Admittedly, I resisted repenting at first, but the Lord continued to press in on my heart until the bitterness faded. Through love God's grace eventually overcame my pride. I prayed, asked God for forgiveness and actually felt my transgressions released. I felt free!

You may have heard bitterness compared to drinking poison and hoping someone else will die. In my experience, it is true. Refusing to repent gives way to bitterness and does more harm to the offended than the offender. It may seem unfair and probably is, but grace trumps fairness.

If sin were judged fairly, where would you be right now? Are you struggling with a difficult time repenting for something today? If so, consider embracing the power of God's grace. Start by giving thanks for the gift of salvation and give room so Christ can do a good work in you.

Looking back I am thankful the church was not lax about dealing with sin. It helped me mature as a believer.

Today, I am happy to report that Britt and I are happily married with our first child, Roman, whom we absolutely adore and cherish. My hope and prayer is that our story will be a reflection of Christ's abounding love and grace so that many will come to know His name.

Brittany Rust is a writer, speaker and pastor at Red Rocks Church in Colorado. A contributor to Propel Women, Crosswalk, iBelieve, YouVersion and *Single Christianity* magazine, she also hosts the Epic Fails podcast. Her passion is to give encouragement to the world-weary believer through her writing, speaking and podcasting. Brittany and her husband, Ryan, have a handsome son named Roman, and together they live with a hyper lab in Castle Rock, Colorado. Learn more at www.brittanyrust.com.